One-Way Ticket Home

A Novel Based on a True Story

K.C. Hardy

One-Way Ticket Home is a novel based on true life events. However, characters, places and incidents are used fictitiously in order to protect the identity of those involved. Any resemblance to any persons, living or dead, occupations, or locales is purely coincidental. The authors and publisher do not assume and hereby disclaim any liability to any party for any loss, damage, or disruption caused by similarities or omissions whether such similarities or omissions result from negligence, accident, or any other cause.

To Anna, Cheri and Mindy, who were there for me during my battles with cancer but now, sadly, have lost their own. Your faith and courage was truly an inspiration and will never be forgotten.

> *"It takes a minute to meet a special person, a day to love them, but an entire lifetime to forget them."*
>
> *~Author Unknown*

To women everywhere whose lives have been touched by breast cancer or domestic violence; may you find courage and strength to victoriously navigate the storms of your life.

And last but certainly not least, this book is dedicated to all of our men and women in uniform who so proudly and courageously serve and defend our country. Thank you for your sacrifice and the gift of freedom you've given to us all.

If you would like to contact us, you can do so through our website at kchardy.com. We would love to hear from you.

There is a river in Italy called the Fiumelatte. For centuries, its origin was a mystery to those fortunate enough to bask in its beauty. It appears during the spring rains and disappears in the fall. But every year it comes back, just as strong, beautiful, and mysterious as the year before.

One-Way Ticket Home

1

San Antonio, Texas
June 6, 2008

*I*t happened just as Julie Whitaker turned off the last set of lights in the office. The ever-present amber glow from the receptionist's desk lamp cast long shadows that gave the normally bustling workplace an eerie, ghost-like feel. Always the last to leave, she stayed long after coworkers had darted off to cart their kids to soccer practice or squeeze in last-minute runs to the grocery store. Having successfully raised two independent daughters, Julie no longer had such obligations. There were no children to pick up from school, drive to soccer, piano, or basketball. There was no husband who expected her to have dinner hot and ready when he walked through the door. She answered to no one...that is, except Clark O'Brien, her boss, mentor, and friend for the past ten years.

And Julie liked it that way—the freedom...the independence...the idea of being able to jet off on exotic vacations whenever she pleased. An idea that always enticed her but which she never had acted upon. Ironically, there still was no time for such luxurious pursuits. There were interviews and database checks at the court house. Deadlines and court dates always loomed. Which was exactly why the grating, high-pitched ring of the phone was even more irritating than usual.

It could only be coming from one place—her desk. She could ignore it, activate the alarm, turn the key in the deadbolt, walk the twelve steps to her car, and be done with work for the next fourteen days. Or...she could answer it. Julie knew who was on the other end of the line. Just before shutting down her computer, she'd shot off a last-minute email to Clark. The message was short, and should have come as no surprise.

> *Clark,*
> *The Sanchez case has been completed and sent to the D.A.'s office. I'm shutting down my computer after I finish typing this and will see you in two weeks. The offer still stands for you and Jodi to join our family in*

*Italy if you would like. Let me know, and I'll overnight
the tickets to you.*
   Ciao,
   Julie

Why couldn't she just ignore the ringing like any other
rational person on the eve of their first vacation in over
two years? Why?

Dedication. The trait that had helped guarantee her
job during the recent string of layoffs was now irritating her. She zigzagged across the room, dodging cubi-
cles that impeded a straight shot to her office. Defiantly
determined not to be here a single minute longer, she
didn't bother switching on the light in her office, much
less sit down. Breathless, she answered the phone before
voicemail picked up.

"This better be good, Clark, because my vacation actually started three hours ago!"

"Then what the heck are you still doing at work,
Whitaker?"

She almost dropped the phone and had to smother
the gasp of shock that made her knees buckle. It wasn't
Clark. There was no mistaking that deep husky voice that
sent her heart pounding and her head reeling from the
instantaneous churning of emotions. It was a voice she
hadn't heard in over twenty years.

"Jules, you there?"

Running her tongue over her lips to both lubricate and pry them apart, she answered his question with a question of her own.

"Mark. What a surprise! How'd you get my number?"

Working as a private investigator, Julie knew how easy it was to locate anyone, anywhere. And if she was being perfectly honest with herself, she'd secretly longed for this call. Yearned for this somewhere inside the most private chambers of her heart. The lack of closure had left a gaping wound that hemorrhaged for years deep within her soul. A casualty that resulted from the swift, premature severing of their relationship. Forcing emotions and memories to be buried so deep, only Roberta Flack's sultry voice, late-night showings of *Top Gun*, or the familiar, nostalgic, musky scent of his signature cologne could unearth them. Still, a part of her wondered: why now? Why after all this time?

"How are you doing?" Julie mustered in the most nonchalant voice possible.

"No complaints. And you?" Typical Mark Jennings. He could've been in a Tomcat, taking fire from all directions, and if someone would have asked how he was doing, he would've responded "piece of cake." It was part of what made him so good at his job.

"I'm doing great."

He cleared his voice. "So you're into the Sherlock Holmes thing now, huh?"

"Yep...gotta keep an eye on everyone like you out there," she teased.

"I bet you make one heck of a private eye."

"You're darn right I do," she laughed. "What about you? You still flying with the Navy?"

"Still flying. But now I'm with American. Been with them nine years. In fact, that's why I'm calling. I bid the San Antonio run at the end of the month and was wonderin' if you'd like to meet up for dinner? For old times' sake?"

Typical Mark, cutting right to the chase. She knew what she should say, what she had rehearsed saying over the years, if this opportunity ever came along again. The phone call from him twenty years ago unraveled the cocoon she so carefully and meticulously constructed. The sound of his voice sent years of therapy, healing, and pieces of her splintered heart swirling erratically into oblivion.

Twenty years ago she had every reason to say no. Back then there was too much to lose. But now things were different. And yet, for some unknown reason, Julie found herself hesitating.

"I don't know if that's such a good idea, Mark..." She couldn't believe her own words even as they left her lips. Every part of her yearned to see him. To get lost in his hypnotic eyes and run her hands through his unruly, thick, sandy hair. She yearned to trace her fingers across his full lips and down his toned arms.

He was quiet for a moment. "What have you got to lose?" he asked, breaking the silence as if reading her thoughts.

Everything, she wanted to say. This time there was no longer a marriage, a husband, or children—lives that could be ruined. All the reasons for not meeting him before no longer applied. And yet she wavered, for the one life that could still be ruined was her own.

"I'll think about it, Mark."

"That'll work I guess."

Suddenly, she was anxious to cut the conversation short before she was reduced to the vulnerable woman who still lurked inside. Even decades later, Julie feared succumbing to the seductive charm of the man who somehow always managed to make her weak in the knees. "Mark, can I get back to you? I'm not trying to cut this short, but I was actually about to leave—"

"For vacation. I gathered that," he laughed but with zero mirth. She sensed a tinge of annoyance creep into his voice.

"I thought you were my boss."

"Wow! You must be really comfortable with your boss!"

"I am." Julie knew Mark well enough to know exactly what he was insinuating, that her relationship with Clark must extend beyond business. It couldn't be further from the truth, but she decided to let him squirm a little in the realm of the unknown.

"Well, think you could have an answer for me when you get back?"

"Sure...I'll let you know in two weeks."

"*Two weeks*?"

"I'm going to Italy for my younger daughter's wedding."

"Your three year-old's getting married?" he teased.

"My *twenty-six year-old* is getting married."

He let out a long whistle. "Time certainly flies, doesn't it?" His voice took on a somber tone.

"Does it ever!" Julie sighed, nostalgic. It was a sentiment she had felt a lot lately—one that had sent her to Sam's on more than one occasion to stock up on economy packages of Kleenex.

"Jules..."

"Yeah..."

"I really hope we can meet up..."

She didn't say she hoped so too. "I'll call you when I get back. And thanks for calling. It's great hearing from you."

"Be safe over there."

"I will...thanks."

Julie sank deeper into the chair after putting down the receiver. The blinking green light on the laptop bounced off the beige walls in the dark room, sporadically illuminating the framed pictures of her girls. Baby pictures. Pictures of them riding their first bikes. Pictures of their proms. Identical pictures taken at their graduation from the University of Texas with the tower lit up behind them amidst a sea of fireworks. There were so many accomplishments, milestones, other loves, and other losses. She had lived a life largely without looking back. Mostly free of regrets.

That is, except for one....

2

Varenna, Italy
June 9, 2008

Three days later Julie found herself sandwiched between mounds of luggage on a rickety bus as it forged ahead through the Italian terrain. The open windows whipped up a cool breeze that danced through her blonde, shoulder-length, straight-as-an-arrow hair. Throughout her adolescence, Julie had envied Billy-Jean Briley and her fiery auburn curls that seemed to bounce in the sunlight, mirroring her bubbly personality. The old cliché rang true—we always want what we can't have.

It was three o'clock in the afternoon, exactly five days and two hours before her younger daughter would be getting married. The wedding had consumed every waking minute of her days and many sleepless nights. The Type A personality that made Julie successful in her professional life had certainly come in handy for Zoe's wedding. Every *i* had been dotted, every *t* meticulously crossed. And she'd enjoyed every minute of it, from sifting through bridal magazines with Zoe late at night in their pj's to deciding which champagne to serve for the toast. Julie soaked it all in, savoring every moment they shared—knowing this momentous event would pass all too quickly.

The plane had landed in Milan less than two hours ago. Julie had always envisioned Italy as the quintessential setting for medieval star-crossed lovers, where Romeo and Juliet met their timeless fate. Where the faded white marble of ancient Roman ruins dotted the landscape, where the Leaning Tower of Pisa seemed to sway by the breeze, where gondolas meandered down the sleepy canals of Venice and sun-drenched meadows delighted the eyes and saturated the senses.

Gazing out the window, she looked with wonder at the ribbons of citrus, pine, and eucalyptus trees that spread across the unspoiled countryside. Colorful wildflowers were springing up in joyous abundance, bathing the hills in pink, yellow, and white. *Now this is more like it,* she thought, adjusting her over-sized sunglasses and leaning back into the well-worn upholstered seat.

"Mom!" Zoe's voice shot up from the back of the bus. "How much longer to Varenna?" Her daughter peered over the top of the seat, scrutinizing her mother. Zoe never missed a thing. Ever. A trait that suited her well at her job with the FBI but still irritated the living daylights out of her family.

With a quick glance over her shoulder, Julie found herself looking at a six-year-old girl with her brown hair pulled up in pigtails that framed her small face. Dimples flashing a smile that revealed two missing front teeth. Now look at her. Her brown wavy locks, sun-kissed golden skin that always looked as if she'd just returned from the beach and hazel green eyes had helped her land a part-time modeling gig in college. Sometimes she found herself missing her precocious, active child who'd always kept her on her toes.

"I'm not sure, hon. The map's inside my luggage," she said with a nod toward the suitcases precariously stacked nearby.

"Never mind then," she said with a shrug, turning back to her fiancé. Zoe had sworn it had been love at first sight when she'd first caught a glimpse of Travis, the tall boy with a military style buzz haircut, in a criminal defense class her junior year at the University of Texas. She'd brought him home for Thanksgiving that year and the rest was history. He was good for her Julie mused, watching Travis plant a soft kiss on Zoe's forehead. He was the calming force in Zoe's life. And her daughter's vivacious, boundless energy helped him come out of his self-imposed shell.

At times Julie still found it hard to believe that Zoe had grown into this beautiful twenty-six-year-old woman who was about to be married. Where had all those years gone? Only yesterday she'd been asking her whether she wanted a peanut butter or turkey sandwich in her sack lunch, and suddenly the question had changed to what color she wanted her bridesmaids' dresses to be.

Julie would have typically shared these moments with her mom. God, how she missed her...especially now. She wanted to talk to her, sit next to her, hear her voice, and share a laugh. They'd recall the time when Zoe put potato chips down her diaper, or hid Hershey's Kiss wrappers in every nook and cranny of their home. What words of wisdom would her mother have offered up now? The fact that neither of her parents was alive to see their grand-daughter get married was a painful reality. Two integral parts—the irreplaceable pieces of a puzzle—were missing.

"*Benvenuti*, Varenna. Everyone-uh, welcome to-uh, Varenna." Their driver struggled shamelessly through a thick Italian accent to spit out his broken English.

Conversations abruptly stopped as everyone craned to get a closer look at the town they'd only seen in travelers' photos from TripAdvisor.com. The ancient fishing village looked almost magical as its image reflected atop the vast silky blue waters of Lago de Como. Narrow alleyways wound their way on determined paths to the lake.

The weathered yet colorful cluster of buildings clung to each other and to the shoreline as though avoiding being swallowed up by the shadow of the mountains that rose behind them. Brilliant red geraniums spilled over pots and window boxes while bougainvilleas climbed the buildings and azaleas towered like trees. Julie stood there for a moment, mesmerized.

The quaint hotel, with its emerald green shutters and aged stone, was situated invitingly along the water's edge. Gas lanterns flickered on either side of the double French doors. A weathered sign with the words "Benvenuti Amici — Welcome Friends" swung freely over the entrance. Pausing in the doorway, she took one last look at the sprawling lake that stretched before them. Evening rapidly approached as the sun started setting over the Alps, painting the sky with hues of crimson, orange and pink. Only remnants of snow that gracefully covered the mountains during the winter months remained. White sails of several boats sparkled like diamonds against the rich blue lake.

Thirty-four minutes and twenty-two pieces of luggage later, everyone was checked into their rooms. They'd heard about the famous lack of charm that was characteristic of many European hotels, so the small balcony that offered an awe-inspiring view of the lake came as a pleasant surprise. Tossing her purse onto the bed and kicking off her shoes, Julie stepped onto the terrace. The stone felt cool and damp under her bare feet. She plopped down on the white wrought-iron chair as if it were her favorite worn-out reading chair back home. Her body was too tired to notice the difference. The water glimmered like liquid gold for a few moments as the sun slowly sank below the horizon.

Without the cumbersome luggage in tow, she was finally able to soak in the panoramic views. A sailboat docked at the ferry landing about half a mile or so away. She couldn't help but wonder how many others had sought refuge or inspiration on the shores of Varenna. Evening gave way to night and the golden rays from the sunset faded into the flickering nighttime lights of Varenna. A cool tropical-like breeze brushed gently across her face.

Reasons abounded why she shouldn't be here. She thought of pivotal points in the timeline of her life where even the most brilliant physicians would most likely have written her off. And yet, every time she had dug in her heels and defied the odds, refusing to become a part of some conventional narrative of how her life "should" play out.

The full moon rose slowly, occasionally peaking from behind the clouds to bathe the lake in its trail of light. She found herself replaying the conversation with Mark over and over in her head. She recalled the breathless excitement that colored his voice. The heightened curiosity of why he had called in the first place. There was so much he didn't know. They had been so young. So crazy in love. But the years had brought with them many changes...changes he knew nothing about.

The romantic setting played out like a Shakespearean sonnet all around her. Julie's mind went back thirty-six years, to a time and place when the stars held the bright promise of her tomorrows in their hands. It was a love that captured the very essence of who she was, and who she would become...

3

Austin, Texas
1972

Bell-bottomed jeans, fringed leather belts, and Credence Clearwater Revival heralded the dawn of a new generation. Free love, liberation and psychedelic exploration had invaded college campuses from coast to coast. The year was 1972, and I was eighteen and a sophomore at the University of Texas at Austin. Just because you had been "somebody" in high school didn't mean you were going to be "anybody" here. This became a sobering reality check for many unsuspecting freshmen, myself included. So the little free time I did have was divided between hanging out with my roommates and singing in one of the University's choral groups. It was during one of the performances with the Southern Singers that I would meet him.

The first time I saw him, I really didn't see him. I sensed him. I sensed his eyes staring a hole through me. When he smiled, the boy with piercing blue eyes was the only face I saw in the sea of cadets. Everyone else faded into the background as we sang "California Dreamin". As if overtaken by some mystic gravitational force, every few seconds, my gaze was drawn in his direction. Yet a stab of guilt gnawed at me. But why? I was sure I hadn't really been flirting with him. Or had I?

After the performance, I surveyed the endless spread of hors d'oeuvres, only half-listening to Sue chatter on about her ragweed allergy and her disdain for anything pimento, when a deep voice interjected from behind me, "Pink always has been my favorite color."

Startled, I turned to find the same cadet whom I had exchanged teasing glances with only minutes earlier. Standing there in his crisp white uniform and donning a slow grin that spread across his chiseled face, he looked even more handsome up close. And those eyes! Their intensity stirred in me both discomfort and excitement at the same time. His movie-star looks could reduce even the most confident woman into a giddy star-struck teenager. The blood rushed to my face and my cheeks flushed with warmth.

Observing my puzzled look, he pointed to my dress. "That *is* pink, isn't it?"

Recovering, I met his gaze, laughed, and retorted with a coy smile, "Well, yes it is. But somehow I find it hard to believe it's *your* favorite color."

"Why's that? Don't you know that only *real* men love pink?" he laughed.

There was no doubt that the guy standing in front of me was indeed a *real* man—a hunk in every sense of the word. I could picture him as the star athlete from his high school, a hunter on the weekends, and someone who had never visited a repair shop because he knew how to fix everything himself. And I was equally confident that pink was *not* his favorite color.

"Mark. Mark Jennings," he said, taking a step forward and extending his hand toward mine.

"Julie Whitaker," I managed to say in spite of the lump in my throat. His handshake was firm. His grip—strong. Daddy always said you could tell a lot about a man from his handshake.

"Nice to meet you, Julie Whitaker," he said, my name rolling off his tongue in a tantalizing manner.

"Likewise, Mark Jennings." Silence stretched before us as I hesitated, my mind in overdrive while trying to manage a remotely intelligent response. *It doesn't have to be brilliant. Just something. Anything!*

"Well, Julie Whitaker, your group was sure a hit with the guys."

"Thanks. Glad you enjoyed it." The charged air between us was so palpable I could practically touch it. The feeling of exhilaration. Suffocation that makes one light in the head, clouding one's thoughts, tying one's tongue.

Mark inched closer to me so he could be heard above the growing crowd congregating around the assortment of sandwiches and asked in a slightly louder tone, "Would you mind giving me your number so I could call you sometime?"

My heart stopped. The "I'm sorry but I already have a boyfriend" response somehow got caught in my throat. *Shoot!* There were those eyes again, hypnotizing me into submission. Charming. Handsome. Confident with a dose of aggressive bravado stirred in for good measure. An intoxicating cocktail that should have turned me off at the onset. But it didn't: I was already hooked.

So instead, I nodded, smiled, and let out an all too eager, "Sure, I'd like that!"

Reaching into his pocket, he whipped out his program and a pen. "Then how 'bout an autograph, Julie Whitaker?"

Our fingers brushed momentarily as I took the pen and jotted down my number.

"Thanks. I'll give you a call then," he said, flashing one final irresistible grin.

"Sounds good," I said, smiling back.

"See you around, Julie Whitaker," he said with a wave of the program, before turning and walking away.

I stood there watching him wondering what I had just done.

The image of Tom, my high school sweetheart, flashed brilliantly in my mind like a neon sign. His class ring hung loosely around my neck underneath my dress. Sweet, romantic, Tom, who thought nothing at all of driving up to Austin two, sometimes three days a week.

We had gone "steady" since my sophomore year of high school. Ever since my mother, ignoring my barrage of relentless pleading, had signed me up for ballroom dance lessons at the Evelyn Moore studio across town. But, three lessons into the six-week course, a tall cute boy with chocolate brown eyes and hair to match soon had me thanking her. That's how Tom and I started— as dance partners in a stale smoky room surrounded by ten other awkward teenage couples, learning everything from the foxtrot to the Viennese waltz. At the time, I was on my high school's dance team and Tom was a star football player for our arch rivals, the Marshall Mustangs. He adored me. The feeling was mutual. Our relationship had survived four years at different high schools and a handful of other interested suitors on both our parts.

I tugged at the gold cross necklace that hung entangled with Tom's class ring. Looking back, I couldn't help but think that those evenings at the dance studio were a rite of passage in so many ways. Each uncertain step taking me farther and farther away from the days of my childhood. So why then did I find myself caught in this sudden flirtation with some random stranger?

"Who on earth was *that* hunk?" Sue asked mischievously, interrupting my reproachful thoughts. With eyebrows raised and lips pursed, she expressed both surprise and amusement at this delicious new development. Sue, with her insatiable curiosity, was busy retying the oversized lavender and white polka-dotted bow draped around her signature ponytail. It was a welcome distraction from the line of questioning that was sure to follow.

At 5'11", Sue towered over my 5'6" frame. She'd been valedictorian of her class and a star basketball player in the small Missouri town where she'd grown up. She briefly toyed with the idea of playing for Texas but wisely decided against it. Her challenging pre-med schedule wouldn't allow much time for extracurricular activities, and so she opted for the much less strenuous Southern Singers instead. Our opposite personalities complemented each other. The new friendship eased the twenty-minute daily treks to and from the music hall. Right now, though, her warm brown eyes bore down on me in a way that was disconcertingly similar to the way my eighth-grade science teacher's had when I'd been caught passing notes.

"I want every juicy detail, Julie Elizabeth," she said, her hands demandingly settling on her hips.

I smirked. She could suffer for a little while longer. After all, someone asking for your number is hardly considered *juicy*. Meanwhile, thoughts of Tom lurked around in my head like a haunting tune you hear on the radio in the morning whose notes you're still humming that evening.

"Well...whoever it was, he sure seemed to be all googly-eyed over you," Sue smiled playfully as she looped her arm through mine. We headed back to our dorm, swishing the autumn leaves along the way.

That evening, as the girls reminisced excitedly about all the handsome cadets in the crowd, I couldn't help but think about Mark. The swarm of emotions that invaded my body was raw and unfamiliar. I didn't know I could feel this way. But I could almost hear my daddy's voice of reason: *Slow down, Julie. Don't go puttin' the cart before the horse.* He would be right. He usually was. All this worrying and Mark might not even call. But every single solitary cell in my body desperately wanted him to.

4

Varenna, Italy
June 9, 2008

"Mom...you comin' down for dinner?" Jason, Julie's son-in-law's voice jolted her back to the present. The handsome 6'4" man still reminded her of the tall, lanky high school sophomore who'd grown up next door and stolen her older daughter's heart. She'd watched their sweet friendship slowly evolve over time—hours of cut-throat games of basketball and ping pong—had at some point blossomed into something more. He'd become a fixture in the Cortisi household ever since. More like a son than a son-in-law.

"Y'all go on ...I'll be there in a second," Julie said, swinging her legs over the side of the bed.

"Okay, see ya down there." His voice trailed off and the sound of his footsteps echoed off the tile floor, growing fainter and fainter.

Julie traipsed to the bathroom for a quick touch-up. The splash of cool water rejuvenated her. An inadvertent glance in the mirror...and a familiar reflection—high, dominant cheekbones that told the story of her father's Cherokee lineage were a youthful trademark that transcended time. And in spite of the faint lines around her eyes, she'd had the genetic good fortune of aging well. A quick reapplication of Revlon's barely-there lipstick and a few strokes of L'Oreal's cotton-candy blush and *voila,* she once again was transformed into a fresh-faced mother of the bride.

Mother of the bride! The phrase alone made her cringe. Even though she'd been down this road once before, she still had trouble swallowing the matronly title. And yet, it was a badge of honor she should have been wearing with pride. And she *was* proud! Proud of both her daughters for the beautiful women they'd become. Proud of the role she'd played in shaping them. And she felt blessed and thankful to be here for this day.

So, why this aching inside? This bewilderment at exactly where the twenty-six years had gone? Sometimes, she still felt like the eighteen-year-old girl who had fallen hard for the Navy cadet all those years ago. The girl who never missed the opportunity to dance barefoot to "Bad Moon Rising" with her long hair flowing in the wind. The days seemed as though they would last forever. That was one of the mysterious trademarks of time—it has a way of standing still, yet flying by almost simultaneously. She couldn't have possibly known how quickly the years would disappear.

Zipping up the make-up case and turning the bathroom lights off, her thoughts momentarily drifted back to Mark. *Not now, not tonight.* This was a happy occasion— neither the time nor the place for painful memories of the past. Nothing was going to cast a shadow over Zoe's wedding. And as she shoved the make-up case into her purse, she half-convinced herself that she'd be able to do just that. Not think about *him.*

As was typical for the Cortisi clan, they could be heard long before they could be seen. The hostess escorted her through the ancient Roman-style dining room with its rich warm red hues in the direction of her family's voices. A single rose and two flickering white candles adorned each table. White lights draped the balcony railing below and intertwined with the vines that had grown around the wooden arbor above.

"Glad you could make it," Tony quipped. "You can never be on time for anything."

"Oh Tony, we're in Italy for our daughter's wedding, for crying out loud...stop looking at your watch." He rolled his eyes in mock exasperation and resumed his conversation with Jason.

Her ex-husband had been an excellent father. He was a pilot, which meant more time apart than together. But that hadn't bothered Julie. She'd grown independent. Strong and self-reliant. But like every woman, she needed to know that she was appreciated, loved, and missed when he walked back through the door at the end of a long trip. A hug. A kiss. An "I missed you" would've been nice. But that never happened. As the years passed, the distance between them, geographically as well as emotionally, made it harder to bridge the loneliness. Their conversations eventually came to revolve solely around the girls' sporting events and school work. Fluff dialogue that never managed to delve beneath the surface. It became harder and harder to feel connected with him, not only when he was away, but when he was sitting directly across the kitchen table from her.

Julie contemplated all of this while Tony threw his head back in laughter at something Jason said. His hearty laugh that resonated from deep within was contagious, even addictive. And just as Mark's self-assured, blatant desire for her had drawn her in like a moth to a flame, Tony's persona and unencumbered laughter became the glue that had cemented her attraction to him. For a while, that had been enough. More than enough. But over time, apathy and indifference settled over their marriage like a dark mist slowly being absorbed to the point of saturation. Phone calls became cold, impersonal, and strained. Short. So short that she'd been compelled to search his flight bag for any possible explanation. Anything that might explain what he himself was unwilling to. Hours of therapy only led to years of denial, frustration, and heartache. And ultimately, the death of another dream.

But the girls had been the bond that tied them together over the past fifteen years. And their relationship settled into a place of acceptance. Acceptance of each other's weaknesses and differences. Free of the typical demands and sometimes unrealistic expectations, they redefined their relationship into something even better—friendship.

The waitress arrived with water and glasses of wine. Swirling the Chardonnay around in the tall-stemmed glass, she felt herself beginning to unwind.

Zoe and Allie had been lucky in love, but a small part of Julie wanted to hang on to the yesterdays of their childhood. Zoe was the baby. The younger of two children she was never supposed to have. A diagnosis of endometriosis at the age of seventeen and years of operations, tests, and visits to specialists had informed her that she had a one-in-a-million chance of ever conceiving a child. She'd grown to accept the idea that children were simply not in the cards for her. But now, sitting on either side, were the two greatest blessings of her life. How thankful she was that all the doctors had been wrong. They were, after all, the better parts of her.

Following a very traditional Italian fare befitting of their first night in Italy along with several rounds of both

humorous and sentimental toasts, everyone retired early.
The long flight had taken its toll. Forty-five minutes and
what seemed like a pound of cannoli and pirogues later,
she had her shoes off and eyes closed. The events of the
day swirled around like the ceiling fan circling above. In
the calm of the evening, once again, as hard as she tried
not to, thoughts of Mark unwittingly invaded her mind.

5

Austin, Texas
1972

Sue poked her head around the corner and hissed, "Jules, why on earth are you in here?" Her face squinched unconsciously in disgust and her incredulous tone balked at the audacity of studying on such a gorgeous day.

"Come with us, we're heading to Barton Creek."

"I wish, Sue, but I can't."

Sue didn't ask why. She already knew why. She had warned that I was nuts to take Anthropology on a full schedule, but I thought she was exaggerating as always. Woefully, I was beginning to realize she wasn't. Mercifully, Sue decided not to rub it in my face. "Okay, well if you change your mind, you know where to find us!"

The fall semester had barely begun and already I found myself secluded on a picture-perfect Saturday afternoon in one of the solitary, jail-cell-like rooms of the library, trying my best to read chapters four, five, and six from Anthropology 302. A situation I usually didn't find myself in until crunch time right before finals. As Sue's willowy figure disappeared among the rows of bookshelves, I ran my hand through my hair for what seemed like the hundredth time while staring at the same sentence from the same chapter of the same book. Thoughts from the evening before clouded my mind, impeding my efforts to study. And Sue, Patsy, and Lori splitting for an afternoon of fun in the sun didn't help my lack of focus either. In no time at all, she and the girls would be lathering on their first coat of baby oil and iodine on the banks of Barton Creek while surreptitiously checking out the cute college guys from behind the safety of their obscured sunglasses.

Pounding my head on the book, I let out another exaggerated sigh that bounced off the barren walls of the claustrophobic room. The sigh that if I was at home would have prompted the response, "You throwin' yourself a pity party, Julie Elizabeth?" from my mom. Slamming the book triumphantly shut, I decided to adopt the "if you can't beat 'em, join 'em" attitude and proceeded to march out of the library, down the steps, across the street, and through the double doors of Jester dorm to grab my swimsuit.

Taped to the edge of the bulletin board was a note from Dottie, my roommate: *Julie, some guy named Mark called — CA2-3851. He wants you to call him back.*

Clutching the piece of paper to my chest, I tilted my head up toward heaven in a fervent prayer of gratitude and fell backward on the bed, my feet dangling slightly off the side. And still, feelings of guilt over Tom were clamoring their way to the surface once again. Tom. My high-school sweetheart, my first love. But any sense of remorse was swept aside by the pure ecstasy sparked with the words scrawled on the square piece of paper. I waited a few minutes to give my heart time to settle back down, took a few deep breaths, rolled over, and picked up the phone to dial Mark's number.

"Hello," a deep, familiar voice answered.

"May I speak to Mark, please?" I asked, knowing good and well that the unmistakable voice on the other end of the line was his.

"Depends on who's asking," he joked.

"It's Julie. Julie Whitaker."

"Who? Never heard of her!"

Sensing my embarrassment, he swiftly interjected, "Oh wait, you mean the beautiful blonde I met last night... of *course* I remember you."

I laughed nervously. What was it about him that made me feel this way? Yes, he was handsome. But Tom was handsome too. There was something I just couldn't put my finger on, but the very thought of Mark made me light up inside.

"Thanks for callin' me back. I had a question for you. I need a foxy date for the Navy Marine Corp Ball Saturday night. You free?" he laughed, seemingly amused by his own question. "I know it's last minute and if you can't I understand," he continued.

"Sure! That sounds swell," I responded, still reeling from the word foxy.

"Cool!" he said. "Pick you up at seven then."

"Sounds good, see you then," I said after giving him directions to my dorm, somehow concealing my sheer euphoria.

I placed the phone back on the cradle, and looked out the rectangular dorm window. On a clear day in Austin, Texas, I could see all the way down Congress Avenue to the Capitol. But today was no ordinary day. Today I could see even further. I could see forever with Mark Jennings.

But a wave of guilt crashed over me as I once again read the note from Dottie, this time more slowly, realizing that in all my excitement I hadn't noticed the P.S. scribbled at the bottom: "Tom called too," punctuated at the end with a comically large exclamation point complete with Dottie's signature heart. Even though I knew Dottie always replaced her dots with hearts, at this moment it felt like a cruel joke, and I envisioned her bearing down on her pencil as she wrote the note, judgment spilling onto the paper with every word. Dottie was well aware of Tom, and I would have quite of bit of explaining to do when she returned.

Right now though, Dottie was the last thing on my mind.

For the next few hours I struggled with what to say to Tom. I didn't want to lose him, but it wasn't fair to keep him hanging on. He deserved to find someone who was as crazy about him as I already was about Mark. He deserved honesty and truthfulness.

So, at nine o'clock that night, as twilight deepened outside the window of my room, I reluctantly broke things off with Thomas Edward Williamson III, severing a four-year relationship, to take a chance on a mysterious stranger.

Forty-eight hours and what seemed like one hundred dress boutiques later, with the help of my two most trusted allies, I found *it*. When just about to give up all hope, I had spotted the rose-colored dress in the display window of Deco's, a small boutique on the drag.

"That's it, Sue!" I shrieked. "That's the dress!"

Sue reached for the tiny crucifix she'd worn around her neck since her thirteenth birthday, clutched it tightly,

K . C .   H A R D Y

whispered a short prayer, and momentarily glanced up to the heavens. "*Please* have that dress in her size!"

Being a good Catholic girl, Sue was known to always ask for help from above when faced with a daunting task. Unbeknownst to me, the dress hunt had fallen into this category. She whispered the same short prayer during one of the many all-nighters we had pulled for chemistry.

Sue's prayer worked, however, and now here I stood in front of the full-length mirror, amazed that a last-ditch effort could be such a perfect fit.

"Wow," Dottie remarked as I finished applying one more coat of pink frenzy lip gloss and smoothed out the rose-colored dress. "Where are you going all dolled up?"

With her brash persona, my roommate was not known for her tactfulness. She was, however, known for her un-wavering attempts at garnering attention from the male side of our dorm. On more than one occasion, Dottie had scribbled our phone number on the laundry room window—her sexy, raspy voice served as a magnet that drove guys wild. But most evenings she could be found curled up on the twin bed, winding the black cord from the phone around her fingers like a snake roping in its prey. I'd come to realize that Dottie was all talk, though. Her phone rendezvous masked a low self-esteem. In our two years as roommates, she never once mustered up enough courage to actually meet a single guy.

I had been hoping that she would be at one of her study groups, or otherwise distracted in one of her illicit phone calls. But nope, there she was parked on her bed, her small round eyes narrowing inquisitively, wondering what I was up to.

"I'm going to the Navy ROTC Ball," I responded, hoping she wouldn't be interested in the details. No such luck.

"The Navy ROTC Ball?" she repeated, mouth agape. "When did all this happen? Obviously, you aren't going with Tom..."

"Not now, Dottie. I'm running late." A twinge of guilt knotted in my stomach. After a year of being stuck in such close proximity to someone, you get to know them pretty well. And I knew that any time Dottie fidgeted with that orange and white afghan her grandmother had crocheted for her that she was upset. Maybe I shouldn't have been so short.

"I'll fill you in on everything when I get back, okay? Promise."

"Fine. Well, I'm going with a couple of girls to the Bucket, so guess I'll just talk to you later then," she muttered, followed by an unenthused, "Have fun."

"You too," I said as she closed the door behind her.

My long blonde hair down to my waist parted simply in the middle was always easy to fix. A quick splash of Shalimar on my wrists was the perfect finishing touch. I was determined to arrive downstairs before he did.

Two thunderous knocks rattled the door.

Dottie had probably forgotten something.

I walked across the room, slightly irritated that she had once again refused to look for her key, knowing good and well I was trying to get ready for my date. Opening the door, I was startled to see Mark in his starched white Navy uniform, holding a single rose in his right hand and clutching his Navy hat in his left.

I froze in disbelief and felt as though my heart would literally leap out of my chest. How on earth had he managed to get past our RA, Nancy? She was a stickler for rules and couldn't be swayed by a gorgeous man in uniform...or could she?

"It's beautiful...and pink!" I said.

"Told you it was my favorite color."

We both laughed.

"Have a seat," I said, pointing toward my bed. "I'm almost ready. How did you manage to get up here?" I couldn't help but ask.

"Well, let's just say there were originally two roses in this hand," he laughed.

I knew it. Guess I was wrong about Nancy. Was there anyone who could resist this man's charm?

Mark sat down as I hastily scrambled for something to put the rose in. Even the way he sat down was sexy.

His forearms rested on his upper thighs while he casually searched the room. "Nice place," he said, fiddling with his hat.

"Thanks. It's small, but it works." I looked up in the mirror over the sink as I filled a cup with water only to see Mark staring at the picture of Tom in the gold frame on my desk. Completely mortified, I closed my eyes. Darn! If I had known he'd be seeing my room, I would have stashed that picture in my desk drawer. Too late. I made the snap decision not to mention it unless he did.

"I'm guessing this is my competition?" He nodded in the direction of the frame.

I'd always blushed very easily. One of my traits I loathed. I was an open book in so many ways. My expressions, my eyes, my skin coloring always revealed much more than I intended to divulge. I kept my back to him.

With the water now cascading over the top of the cup, I managed a flimsy explanation in the most nonchalant tone I could, "Oh, it's just this boy from high school." A little too "la-di-da" perhaps, but it seemed to work. Nothing more was said.

$\sim$ $\sim$

"Come on, Julie, let's show 'em how it's done!" Mark playfully taunted, grabbing my hand, wasting no time.

The lights were dimmed. Blue and gold balloons floated high above the tables. A DJ served up the most popular tunes. And a few brazen people were already burning up the dance floor while the more timid couples waited it out on the sidelines. Instantly, I was taken back to my senior prom. And Tom. Of the phone call the day before when I knew I had hurt him. Guilt was once again thrust front and center. I shooed it away and followed close behind Mark.

He was greeted with high fives from several other guys as he whisked me off to the dance floor. I had a brief glimpse of who he'd probably been in high school. Effervescently cool without knowing or trying. A charismatic personality one had to be born with that, when combined with devastatingly good genes, fuses into a person everyone wants to hang out with, and whom girls naturally couldn't resist.

Mark was just as easy to dance with as he was on the eyes. His body moved in perfect rhythm to "Bang a Gong" by T.Rex. Against my better judgment, I found myself getting caught up in the whirlwind of the evening...caught up in Mark Jennings.

"So what's your major?" I asked in an attempt to defuse the intensity building between us.

"I'm in the Navy ROTC program but my major is engineering. Two more years in the program and I'll be an ensign in the U.S. Navy, m'am." He jokingly raised his right hand to his forehead, thrusting his shoulders back while standing at attention, saluting me.

I rolled my eyes. "Wow...smart, brave, *and* good looking. I'm impressed."

"What about you?"

"Not quite as exciting—nursing. Eventually I'd like to specialize in pediatrics or labor and delivery."

"I'd call that brave!" he teased. "Sounds pretty exciting to me."

I laughed.

After a couple of fast songs, we made our way to the refreshment table. I noticed how he poured my punch first and then his. How he pulled out my chair at the table before sitting down himself.

Dr. Allen, my Shakespeare professor, had recently imparted one of his many pearls of wisdom on his less than enthusiastic audience of students when referring to Othello: "Remember ladies, every man has his tragic flaw." He had said it with conviction and certainty, as though he were reciting an uncontestable truth, an algebraic theorem or Sir Isaac Newton's law of gravity. Dr. Allen's words had struck a chord with me. But for now, all I could do was wonder what Mark Jennings' tragic flaw was. He had to have at least one crack in his shiny armor...didn't he?

Mark and I had been talking with his best friend Doug, and Doug's date Tammy, when the band announced the last song for the night. Mark leaned over and whispered in my ear, "May I have this dance?" Just the feel of his warm breath on my neck sent shivers down my spine.

He took my right hand in his left, and put his right arm around the small of my back, pulling me even closer. He pressed his cheek against mine as we floated

effortlessly across the dance floor. Neither of us said a
word as we moved slowly to "The First Time Ever I Saw
Your Face." It was the perfect song, for a perfect moment. It was as though I'd known this man my entire
life. Roberta Flack had never sounded so good.

6

Austin, Texas
1972

He pulled me even closer—so close that I could smell the woody, masculine scent of his cologne...it was intoxicating. *He* was intoxicating. My cheek rested on his shoulder; the stiff cotton material felt firm and solid. I even detected the faint sound of his heartbeat pounding just as fast as mine. He lifted my chin until our eyes met, then leaned down and kissed me with a passion and intensity that I had never known before. Unfamiliar, raw emotions seized me. The music disappeared into the background.

Our lips parted, and he quietly asked, "So, Julie Whitaker...did you have a good time?"

"I had a wonderful time, Mark Jennings," I replied, unable to control the huge smile spreading across my face.

Neither of us noticed the silence that ensued. The song had ended but we continued swaying back and forth. I was living a fantasy straight from the movies, but this was real, and the reality of what was happening was something that even I could not deny.

"Hey Jennings, you two lovebirds gonna boogie all night?" Doug hollered from across the room.

We both turned, startled to find we were the only ones left on the dance floor.

"Man, where'd everybody run off to?" Mark said. Leading me off the dance floor, he asked, "Can I see you tomorrow before I leave?"

"Well....I'll have to check my calendar," I teased. "I'm pretty sure that I can squeeze you in though."

"To what do I owe this honor?" he bantered back, taking hold of my hand.

We walked out to the car, his arm slung around my shoulders. "So where are you going?" I asked.

"Back home to Virginia. He paused as if contemplating what to say next. "My dad hasn't been feeling well. He had some tests run. They're trying to figure out what's going on."

"Oh, I'm so sorry to hear that. I hope he gets to feeling better soon."

"Yah, me too," he muttered. "I'll keep in touch, though. And I should only be gone a few days."

Mark parked the blue Firebird in the Jester parking lot and practically sprinted to the other side of the car to open my door. He reached for my hand and escorted me up the steep hill to my dorm. We had done so much dancing that my feet were killing me. My high-heels were now dangling from my left hand. On this typical fall night, my favorite time of year, orange and yellow autumn leaves occasionally floated down in a whimsical trail from the trees above, crunching underneath my bare feet. The harvest moon, unobstructed by a few wayward clouds, was in its full glory. As was typical for UT, students walked by as if it were five o'clock in the afternoon instead of almost one o'clock in the morning.

Nearing the dorm, my pace slowed, not wanting the night to end. I turned to face him. "I really did have a great time tonight, Mark. Thank you for inviting me."

He paused, briefly opening his mouth as if to say something before abruptly shutting it again. He glanced up toward the sky and exhaled a deep sigh that made his entire chest heave before looking back down at me and saying, "I mean it, Julie. I'll give you a call when I get back." I had no doubt that sincerity was seared in every word.

Our gazes, like our thoughts, lingered. My fingers traced the lining of his uniform jacket, not wanting to let go. A part of me feared that in spite of his reassurance, this might be the last time I would see him. I'd heard horror stories from a couple of my suitemates about guys who made promises they never kept. My mother's words of advice, "The higher you go, the harder you fall," meant to help keep feelings in check, to guard against a myriad of life's disappointments and heartaches, had already fallen on deaf ears.

Taking my shoes from me and dropping them on the ground, he clasped his hands in mine and leaned me back against the brick wall. The light from the streetlamp illuminated his face. Staring intently into my eyes while gently cupping my face with both of his hands, he bent down for one last kiss. In spite of everything I had read from "Dear Abby", and other sundry advice columnists who wrote about the perilous and inherent dangers of kissing on the first date and moving too fast, I found myself jumping—no, diving in head-first.

After that night at the Navy Ball, another two weeks would pass before I would see Mark Jennings again. As Sue had so eloquently put it one night during our long walk home from the music hall, the likelihood of our relationship lasting was not much better than a snowball's chance in hell. After all, he was joining the Navy, she tersely reminded me. An unsuccessful attempt at keeping her best friend's feet firmly planted on the ground.

With each phone call and date we grew closer, our relationship progressing from zero to one hundred seemingly overnight. We did the ordinary things like getting up early to watch the sun rise over Town Lake, as the University rowing team got in their dawn-breaking practice runs. Other times we'd head to Lamar Street for some live music and dancing, our bodies swaying in perfect synchrony beneath the glow of the neon lights. When the weather grew warmer we spread our blankets out across the green banks of Barton Creek, soaking up the sun along with the other well-tanned Austinites while planning the next ten years of our lives. And then there were those times when we did absolutely nothing. Those moments were the ones I cherished the most. We would sit under my favorite maple tree near the bridge behind my dorm while he ran his fingers through my hair. Every stroke sending chills zipping up and down my spine.

I had been upfront with him early on in our relationship, so he knew that if he wanted any children, we would have to adopt. It had taken me months to work up the nerve to tell him about my endometriosis, but all he did was shrug and say, "All I need—or ever will need—is you." And before I could get all sentimental, he had interjected with a devilish grin and a wink, "But...that won't keep us from trying!"

A statement that ended in a partially excited, partially embarrassed, and partially intrigued, but one hundred percent emphatic *not anytime soon*. Mark would always follow with an equally resounding look that was a mixture of surprise, hurt, and mock dejection, clutching his fist to his chest as though I had sent a dagger straight to his heart. He knew where I stood on sex before marriage, but being a typical guy, that didn't mean he'd stop trying, always acting like he was kidding around. But I knew the element of truth that was always lurking just below the surface. In that regard, I called all the shots, and so far I had managed to stay true to my convictions and values.

But in moments of weakness, moments when I drew a sharp breath from the exhilarating feelings pulsing throughout my body, or the way his hand rested on my thigh when he was driving, occasionally giving it a gentle squeeze, I would briefly contemplate why it was again that I was so dead-set against sex before marriage. Conjuring up a mental list of all the reasons why it would be wrong while simultaneously trying to counteract the powerful physical urges of why it would feel so right. But one couldn't erase eighteen years of Christian upbringing, even if the seducer was Mark Jennings.

We discussed where we were going to live; not a tough one, for we didn't have a choice. We simply would end up wherever the Navy assigned him. But, he had confided one evening while we were watching *Blue Hawaii* starring Elvis Presley, he eventually wanted to retire in Hawaii. Fine with me. Anywhere was fine with me as long as I was with him. I loved planning out the future. Our future.

By the time April rolled around, it was undeniable that our relationship had grown beyond the initial no-strings-attached phase and had evolved into something deeper. Mom and Daddy, interested in meeting the person who now occupied most of my time, decided to invite Mark down for Easter weekend. My parents were fiercely protective of both their daughters, but I was particularly worried about Daddy. He was not easily impressed with the boys his little girls brought home. Daddy had given Tom, Eagle Scout and student body president, a hard time in the beginning. Part of me feared that Mark didn't stand a chance.

My fears, however, turned out to be unfounded. As I'd hoped, everyone immediately took to Mark, including Amy, my little sister. And though my dad was a bit more hesitant to fully accept this new man in my life, Mom liked him immediately. Observing the little things, she could tell that he was as crazy about me as I was about him.

By Easter morning, it was evident that he could win over even the most leery of hearts. So the last day of our visit, when my dad shook Mark's hand and said, "It was nice to meet you, son," I knew he genuinely meant it.

I laughed now in retrospect, remembering how anxious I had been and the absurdity of worrying in the first place. Deep down I had known they would love Mark. After all, everyone did.

47

A month later I was on a flight headed to Arlington, Virginia—Mark's hometown. His older brother Steve, an investment banker, and sister-in-law Lori had moved to Lake Anna but would be home for the weekend. And J.R., his younger brother, was still living at home, which as Mark had excitedly exclaimed over the phone two weeks prior meant that I would "get to meet the whole family!" The butterflies were rampant. I knew I wouldn't have a second chance at making a good first impression.

Mark rented a small car at the airport—very small. It looked even smaller, though, with my red leather luggage piled next to it. He effortlessly tossed his duffle bag into the small excuse for a back seat. On the other hand, it took ten minutes, both hands, and numerous rearranging to fit the rest of my luggage in the trunk. I was decidedly grateful that only Mark and I had witnessed this rigorous undertaking.

"You sure you're not planning on moving in with my parents?" he playfully jabbed as he forcefully slammed the trunk shut.

Shielding my eyes from the sun, I retorted, "One can never be too prepared," borrowing what I believed to be a line from the Boy Scout motto. "See what you've gotten yourself into?"

"Well, if you move anywhere, it better be with me," he said, wrapping his muscled arms around me.

Being with Mark felt so good. So warm. Safe. For a moment I forgot why I was here. About the unnerving task that lay in front of me. He pulled back, planting a soft kiss on my forehead before turning to open my car door, unknowingly showing off his toned physique visible beneath the slightly snug polo I had given him for his birthday. Normally not the polo type, he looked uncomfortably handsome and had no doubt worn the shirt solely for my benefit. I smiled. The shirt was turning out to be the gift that kept on giving. Temptation woven in every thread.

Leaving the congestion and noise of the city behind, I felt myself starting to unwind as I stared out the window. "Wow! This is beautiful, Mark!" I hollered over the noise of the radio and the rush of the wind through the cracked windows. The grass was lush and verdant. Flowers lined the medians like it was the first day of spring, instead of the beginning of summer. A welcome contrast to the hot, desolate climate I had left behind in Texas.

"Yeah, it is!" he replied with his boyish grin.

His broad hand was placed slightly higher on my thigh than normal. Electrifying waves surged throughout my body. "You never told me it was this pretty," I said, gripping the edge of my seat as Mark applied more pressure to the accelerator. His Audubon-style of driving was something I still hadn't gotten used to.

"Guess it's one of those things you take for granted," he yelled back, competing to be heard above the whooshing wind that swirled around us, kicking up my wild strands of hair into an erratic dance around my face. He reached down to fiddle with the dial, flipping through a few radio stations before finally turning it off. "You nervous?"

"A little."

"Don't worry, baby, they're gonna love you," he said, taking hold of my hand and giving it a squeeze.

All too soon, we pulled up in front of the Jennings' home. It didn't take long to realize that Mr. and Mrs. Jennings were high society in Arlington...a little tidbit Mark had failed to mention in our nine-month court-ship, but clearly evidenced in their sprawling colonial-style home set amid two acres of perfectly manicured land. Flowers lined the sidewalk leading up to the majes-tic red double doors of the home.

Mark slowed to a stop in the middle of the circular drive and turned off the car. "Relax, Jules. Everything's copacetic."

"I hope so." A tap on the window startled me.

"Didn't mean to scare you! But are you two going to stay in there all day, or are you going to come out and say hi?" The man's broad shoulders lifted in a slight shrug.

"Dad, this is Julie."

"Nice to meet you, Mr. Jennings," I said, climbing out of the car.

"It's good to finally meet you, Julie, and please—call me Carl." He gave the same strong handshake as Mark. "And son...come on around here and let me get a good look at you."

"Dad, you just saw me a couple months ago," Mark said as he walked around the car.

"Can't a dad just be happy to see his son?" Carl asked while slapping his son on the back.

"It's great to see you too, Dad."

"Let's get you both inside. Your mother doesn't even know you're here yet. I was just checking to see if the mail had come when I saw you pull up."

The inside of the home had an elegance that matched the outside in its tasteful yet subdued decorations. Despite its air of opulence, it didn't feel overly stuffy. After Mark showed me to his room where I would be staying for the next week, he decided to give me a brief tour of his childhood home.

Their library slash study was chock-full of awards and honors bestowed upon his father. Mr. Jennings, a retired captain with the Navy, had an aura of power about him and until recently had still worked in Washington D.C. for the government. In exactly what capacity he had been employed seemed to be a secret closely guarded by his inner circle, of which I was not yet a part. All this new information made the idea of calling him by his first name even more awkward.

After the tour was completed, we joined the rest of his family in the living room. I sank into one of the over-sized chairs that flanked the floor-to-ceiling stone fireplace, having trouble reconciling the fact that the man I loved, the man who did cartwheels on a whim, drank milk straight from the carton, and lived in quarters smaller than their kitchen grew up *here*.

"Hey Mom, I'd like you to meet Julie. Julie, this is my mom." I was prepared to extend my hand for a warm greeting, but instead found myself smothered in a motherly hug. His mom was a regular June Cleaver, straight out of an episode of *Leave it to Beaver*, right down to the perfectly coiffed honey-colored locks, that never seemed to be out of place yet still somehow managed to look soft and natural. An amazing accomplishment, as any woman can attest. She even had a hot-out-of-the-oven apple pie a la mode and freshly brewed coffee piping hot and ready to be served from the second our feet hit their massive foyer. Her jewelry was simple; a gold wedding band, a strand of pearls that subtly accentuated her long and graceful neck, and a turquoise ring on her pinky. She exuded an understated sophistication. Quiet elegance was always intimidating in any situation. I had the feeling that at some point she would surprise me. That she wasn't quite as fragile and perfectly put together as she appeared.

And even that evening, my bed—correction, Mark's bed—was meticulously turned down as though I was a guest in some five-star resort instead of Mark's childhood home. The only thing missing was a truffle placed on my pillow and a handwritten card telling me to "enjoy my stay." But even though their home looked like a spread out of *Southern Living*, and Beverly looked as though she could grace the cover of a Saks Fifth Avenue ad, warmth permeated the house, reminding me of the humble place I called home and the three people who lived there.

Observing the Jennings in between sips of the hot coffee my first morning there, I was surprised to see how much Mark resembled his dad, or "Carl" as he had gently corrected me when I had referred to him as Mr. Jennings for the third time yesterday. "Too much formality!" he had exclaimed in his jovial but firm voice. Though I politely obliged, I was not yet comfortable enough to let the name Carl roll off my tongue in some blasé fashion. He was a handsome man with sharp distinctive features and slightly unruly grey-flecked sandy hair. The same tousled look that made Mark so effortlessly sexy. Occasionally, he would look up from the *Wall Street Journal* long enough to participate in a conversation that no one even realized he was listening to. I knew now exactly what Mark would look like in thirty years—still as handsome as ever.

His mother was constantly baking some homemade bread or muffins the first couple of days we were there. For the first time in my life, I had a hard time buttoning my jeans three days into our visit—a new experience for my normally off-the-charts metabolism and almost Twiggy-like frame. J.R., his younger brother who was still living at home, was the wild-child stereotypical "baby" of the family who had his own way of dressing, his own way of talking, and, much to his family's dismay, own way of thinking. I liked him. Immediately. JR had stayed most of the time secluded in his room with The Who blaring from his record player at an irritating decibel, even for my generous standards.

All the feathered conversations, however, seemed purposefully designed to cover up something. Was it all a ruse? Mark insisted that he had no idea what I was talking about. Did he really not see it? Was it simply another example of my overactive imagination? Irrational fears of a girl trying to impress her boyfriend's family? Subtle sidelong glances Mark's mother exchanged with Carl over the top of her gold-rimmed reading glasses, however, told me otherwise. The question was—what were they hiding?

Mark's parents either had some colossal secret they were keeping from Mark, or they simply didn't care for the woman he had brought home and were secretly plotting her demise. By the third day, I was convinced it was the latter. And it would take a heck of a lot to persuade me otherwise. Which is exactly what Mark had been busy trying to do for the past forty-eight hours. Unknowingly, I had pushed him over the edge. During one of our morning jogs throughout the upper-class neighborhood, he had abruptly turned to me, grabbed me by the shoulders and exclaimed, "Jules, I don't really care what *they* think. You're the only one for me. Nothing's going to change that. Understand?"

I didn't want to ruin the trip midway through it, and his parents did seem to genuinely like me. I just couldn't shake the feeling that they were not being upfront about something. With a flippant nod and a reassuring kiss on his cheek, I dropped the subject, grabbed his hand, and squeezed it tight before continuing down the recently re-surfaced street.

As we rounded Pleasant Valley Drive for the warm-down portion of our jog, a black and white terrier barked fitfully as we encroached closer to his turf. The first day he had stayed in the farthest-most section of his yard, bravely barking behind the safety of his fence and the couple hundred feet that divided us. By day five however, familiarity had begun to set in and that same dog now had his nose pressed in between the slats of the black wrought-iron fence, in a half-bark, half-hello. Picking up a stray twig from the curb, I tossed it several feet behind him and watched as he bounded across the yard like a rabbit, tail beating wildly back and forth at his new friend. We had broken a barrier.

Hmmm…maybe that dog was like the Jennings. Perhaps not the most appropriate comparison, but maybe it wasn't really about *me* but rather the *idea* of me. Of my presence in their home. Maybe they just needed time. I nuzzled closer to Mark as he continued talking, satisfied that I had found the explanation for the disconcerting vibe I had been picking up. Mark kept talking, but I had stopped listening.

"So, what do you think?" he asked, turning toward me.

"About what?"

"About this *weekend*!" he raised his voice on the last word, indicating his annoyance that I had blatantly not been listening to a single word he was saying. And he was right; I had tuned him out from almost the moment he had started talking. Not intentionally, of course. But right now I didn't dare ask "What *about* this weekend?" and instead decided to reply with an elusive, "Sure. That sounds great!"

"Really?" he asked, his full eyebrows raised in complete surprise. "Which part?"

"All of it," I responded with a circular wave of my hand, surprisingly and perhaps unwisely agreeing to whatever he had been talking about earlier.

"Okay then, it's settled. I'll call Steve and tell him to expect two for the weekend!"

"Sounds like a plan!" I gulped. Now I wished I'd been listening. Lori and Steve seemed nice enough, just a little more uptight than I was used to. And their new home on the banks of Lake Anna, from what I gathered from a glance at their Christmas card snapshot affixed to Beverly and Carl's fridge, was even bigger than Mark's parents. A surprising feat for young professionals just starting out, though not unfeasible after spending those first two days with them. Steve, an uptight man, perfectly suited for his job, always seemed to be glued to the house phone, unwilling or unable to let go of his work for even a couple days. Just last night, for the fourth time in two days, I had heard him on the phone securing yet another business deal. I was decidedly grateful that Mark was not, nor would he ever be, like his older brother.

Mark could read me surprisingly well.

"Yeah...I'm not so thrilled either," he laughed. "I knew you wouldn't want to go before I asked!"

"Then why'd you ask?"

"Thought it'd be a chance for you and Lori to bond more. Besides, Mom said they've got a nice place. It's like staying at some fancy bed and breakfast."

I shot him a reproachful look, fully expecting him to break into his typical wise-guy grin. But it wasn't there. He was serious. I thought about the bed turned down, the tip of the toilet paper folded in a triangle, the rolled-up towels in the basket next to the sink in the bathroom that was connected to his room. At *his* house. Oh, the irony.

"We'll have fun. You'll see," he said almost convincingly.

＊　＊

The charming yellow Victorian home with the wrap-around porch was situated right on the edge of Lake Anna. Within hours, I had been able to turn my reluctant, half-hearted spirit of agreement into full-blown excitement. Steve had promised to take us out on the lake, and being an avid swimmer and skier, I loved being anywhere near a body of water. After a full day of water skiing we returned to the house, muscles aching, exhausted and starving.

"Hope you guys came hungry. Lori woke up at the crack of dawn to fix your favorite dish, Mark—deviled eggs and cheese biscuits."

I stole an inquisitive sidelong glance at Mark. I hadn't even known until now that he even liked deviled eggs. I made a mental note to get the recipe from Lori before I left.

After retiring to the back porch, I settled into the white wicker swing that was calling my name. In fact, it was the only thing that didn't look as if it was fresh off the delivery truck. The shabby paint was peeling, and the cushion, although extra comfy with several more layers of padding than your standard variety, looked like it had seen one too many hours of sunlight beating down on its' once brightly colored floral and plaid pattern.

Lori emerged from inside the house carrying a tray of olives, deviled eggs, and cheese biscuits.

"Can I help with anything?" I asked, feeling a twinge of guilt at making a beeline for the swing.

"Sure. There's a pitcher of lemonade on the counter. Would you mind bringing it out?"

"Not at all." Lori's willingness to let me help made me feel more comfortable around her.

In less time than it took for me to retrieve the pitcher, Steve and Mark were heavy into a game of pool. It's amazing how initial perceptions can be so off, I thought, watching Steve as I set the pitcher down on the wrought-iron table. The starched shirt, silk tie, and gold cufflinks had been replaced with a worn-out Beatles t-shirt and faded jeans. Yes, he was a driven man with lofty ambitions that played out in this five-bedroom, four-bath home, but he obviously knew how to let loose and have a good time. Something that was evident in the boat he had pulled out for the day, now parked once again in the third bay of the garage next to the spit-to-shine Harley squeezed in beside it.

"You two! Five minutes can't pass without you both wanting to shoot pool!" Lori laughed. Her waves of red curls, which had been pulled back on the boat, now spilled softly onto her shoulders. Bella, their coal black cat, was curled up on the faded ottoman. The sound of unfamiliar laughter roused her out of her near-comatose state just long enough to lift her head, revealing eyes that were the color of the large fern protruding from the clay pot beside her.

Lori picked up her glass and joined me on the swing. We were quiet for a few minutes, swinging leisurely back and forth, our feet rocking us ever so slightly, as we watched the boys. She had the same far-off look in her eyes that I had grown accustomed to seeing the past several days from Beverly. I repressed the desire to quiz her on the family, tediously searching for random clues as to what they were holding back...if anything at all.

I was glad that I exerted that small measure of self-control, for two minutes later, Lori turned to me and asked in a hushed tone and with a slight nod in the direction of the boys, "So how did he take the news?"

"What news?"

Her brow furrowed and her green eyes clouded over with genuine surprise. "You mean they didn't *tell* him?"

"Didn't tell him what?" I asked, growing impatient with the back and forth questions that delayed any concrete answers.

"About Carl."

"*Mark's* dad?"

"Beverly didn't tell you guys?'

"No."

"They found out two weeks ago he has cancer. Lung cancer."

I gasped. Mark had told me his dad hadn't been feeling well. But he had no idea it could be cancer. Mark adored his father. He was the one who'd followed in his footsteps. Looking at him leaning against the dark paneled wall adjacent to the fireplace, contemplating his next move, my heart sank. Now it all made sense: the sidelong glances, the whispers, and dropped conversations when we entered the room. This was why. And all this time I had thought it was about me. At this moment, I felt utterly foolish and self-centered for mistakenly assuming otherwise.

She continued talking softly, recounting the raspy coughs that just wouldn't go away. And about the numerous doctor visits that always ended in bewildered doctors and confusing diagnosis. The physician would send him home, placing the blame on the stress of his job. It wasn't until an ER doctor ordered a CT scan of his lungs during one of his many trips to the hospital that the inoperable one-centimeter tumor was discovered.

"Someone has to tell him, Lori," I said with an unexpected heaviness. Even though I had just met Mr. Jennings, he already felt like a friend.

"Yes, we do," she replied somberly.

For the second time in my life I felt completely inadequate and at a loss for words. The first time had been when I was thirteen and my best friend's father had suddenly died of a heart attack. No warning. No final words. No goodbyes. I had been asked to stay with my friend and her brother while their mother went to the funeral. And as I had sat there in their living room that warm summer morning, all of us listening to the pendulum swing of the grandfather clock in the foyer, I fought to come up with the right words to fill the stone-cold silence. To help it hurt a little less. At a loss for what to say. Just like I was now.

7

Lake Anna, Virginia
1973

The game wrapped up. Mark pushed back his chair, stretched, hung his pool stick on the rack next to the fireplace, and slowly meandered over to where we were sitting. His gaze fell on his sister-in-law's face. "Everything okay?"

"Mark, there's something we need to tell you," Lori said.

Mark's relaxed countenance was replaced with concern as he pulled the chair over, spun it around, straddling it backwards, and propped his elbows up on top.

"What's going on? You girls just find out there's no Santa Claus?"

Normally that kind of comment would have elicited a roll of my eyes, but now it only made my heart ache even more. A surge of affection for his boyish cluelessness welled inside me, oblivious as he was to the life-changing news he was about to face. I longed to shield him from what he was about to hear.

Without warning, Steve blurted from behind, "We found out last week that Dad has cancer. Can't believe they didn't tell you."

His smile disappeared, replaced by a blank stare. He said nothing. Had Mark even heard him?

But then, in a voice barely above a whisper, Mark asked, "What?"

"I guess they didn't want to hit you with it the second you got into town," Steve said with a shrug.

Lori, shaking her head, stood up, and Steve took her spot. He leaned forward on his elbows, wringing his hands as he filled Mark in on the details. A dark sense of dread penetrated the sun-drenched room.

"It's not possible," Mark said. His head hung down, his eyes stared blankly at the concrete patio. "Not *Dad!*"

And it didn't seem possible. Mr. Jennings was a robust man, like his son. Built like an ox. A picture of perfect health.

Rubbing my hand on his back, I softly whispered, "I'm so sorry, babe, but let's hope for the best." My words

sounded empty and shallow. But I was grasping for anything, desperate to help ease his pain.

The two hour drive home later that evening was heavy
with Mark's invisible struggle to digest his brother's news.
His good-natured persona had abruptly vanished, replaced by a sullen man struggling to come to terms with
what he had just heard. The stoic look on his face, reared-
back shoulders, and steel resolve weren't enough to disguise his grief. The questions churned in the silence.

We got in too late that night for Mark to talk to his
dad. I purposely slept in the next morning and took some
extra time showering to give him a chance to talk to his
parents without an audience. By the time I came downstairs, Mark looked like a new man. As though the bur-
den of the crushing news had been lifted. The ear-to-ear
grin smiling back at me as he passed the orange juice and
muffins was a welcome surprise.

"Good morning, Julie," Mr. Jennings said in a tone
that conveyed he knew that I knew.

"Good morning, Mr. Jenn—"

"Upp...Carl, Julie. Call me Carl."

"Okay, Carl," I said, awkwardly.

"So Steve blew my cover, huh?" he said, crinkling the
newspaper before folding it and retiring it on top of the
two-inch stack of sections already read. He leaned back
in his chair, grabbed his reading glasses, folding them
before placing them down on the table, and said with his
hands behind his head, "Ever since he was knee-high to
a grasshopper, that boy's been awful at keepin' secrets."

"Somebody had to tell me, Dad."

"I know. I was just hoping to wait until you were done with your training. Tell you myself. On my terms. Was that too much to ask?"

"Don't worry, Dad. I'll finish."

— —

The next two years moved at an even faster pace. In May of 1974, Mark kept his promise to his dad and we both graduated from UT. I moved back to San Antonio to accept a nursing position at the Methodist Hospital and Mark moved to Pensacola, Florida to begin his aviation pre-flight indoctrination. Mark's dad ended up needing chemotherapy and according to his mom, the treatments seemed to be working and the doctors were hopeful.

Both of us were busy, so busy that time between visits flew by. Being a nurse in the ER at one of the leading hospitals in the state was very demanding, so it was probably a good thing I wasn't surrounded by too many distractions. And if anyone was a distraction, it was most definitely Mark Jennings.

Nevertheless, I was ecstatic when two months later Mark called to let me know he had been selected to go to Beeville to complete his pilot training. Beeville, Texas. Home of Chase Field Naval Air Station. Population 22,000. Forty-six miles northwest of Corpus Christi, Texas and 988 miles closer to me.

8

Varenna, Italy
June 10th, 2008

If there is one thing Julie knew about herself with one-hundred percent certainty, it was this: she was not, nor would she ever be, a morning person. It was the reason friends and family received most of her emails in the midnight hours, and the reason her neighbors could hear the hum of the vacuum cleaner long after they'd turned in for the night.

Which explained why right now, at six forty-five a.m., she was aimlessly pounding the hotel alarm clock hoping that she'd somehow find the darn snooze button.

The thrill of arriving in Italy after a long day of flying coupled with a glass of vino the night before had taken its toll. Pulling the pillow over her head, she tried in vain to muffle the irksome beeping.

The next forty-eight hours were filled with the usual "touristy" things, which included another trip to the Milan airport to pick up friends and family and a packed itinerary of the must-see attractions listed in the travel guide. From historic churches and leisurely strolls through the meticulously manicured gardens of several villas to the unique shopping experience at the open-air markets of Bellagio, where vendors sold everything from buttons to raw fish. They were determined to see it all.

By the time most of the items on the list had been checked off, it was seven o'clock in the evening. Less than forty-eight hours before the "I do's" and a little over two hours away from the highly anticipated bachelor and bachelorette parties. The wedding party decided to start the evening off at Trattoria's, a popular local restaurant. Trattoria's was known as much for its freshly shaved porcini, parmesan salad and osso bucco with polenta as it was for its lavish wine list. The forty-five minute wait time was longer than anticipated, but as they would discover— well worth it.

Both the girls and guys unanimously decided that karaoke would be a fun way to end the festive evening. The choices in the sleepy lakeside village were extremely limited, however. Nevertheless, the only option, La Divina

Commedia, came highly recommended by the concierge as a perfect after-nine party destination.

The strong smell of smoke billowed into the streets along with the pulsating sound of music from the crowded club.

"Hey, Zoe!" Missy shouted above the noise. "Let's show these Italians how we get down in the States!"

Zoe shook her head in defiance of her friend's wishes.

Julie watched with amusement, knowing that her daughter's protests were too late. Missy was already halfway to the stage, leaning over to ask the DJ a question.

Missy then strutted back to the group with an inflated air of confidence. Missy, a friend of Zoe's since first grade, was a vivacious petite girl with raven hair that fell to her shoulders. The normally angelic face now smirked devilishly at her best friend. Zoe winced apprehensively. Knowing her daughter, Zoe was probably wishing right about now that she had eloped. But it was too late for that.

The familiar opening chords to "Wild, Wild West" vibrated from the stage speakers as the DJ announced the song like an Italian Bob Barker on *The Price Is Right*. "Come on down! Zoe Cortisi! Do we have a Zoe Cortisi here?"

Zoe shrunk even deeper into her chair, covering her face with her hands. She never did like being the center of attention. The room whooped and hollered as locals and tourists alike egged the bridesmaids on as they dragged the reluctant bride-to-be, plastic rhinestone-studded tiara and veil flying behind her, through the crowds and onto the small platform. The DJ handed the girls several microphones and Missy shoved one in front of Zoe.

> *"Forty-seven deadbeats livin' in the back streets, north, east, west, south, all in the same house. She's so mean, but I don't care, I love her eyes, and her wild, wild hair..."*

Soon everyone in the nightclub joined in a rousing rendition of the song, in a mix of both Italian and English. The European tourists' and Italian locals' thick accents didn't hamper their exuberant enthusiasm as they belted out the words to the popular American song. . .the girls were having the time of their lives. The smiling faces, hearty laughter, and pure joy that permeated throughout the group were contagious and spread to other patrons in the bar. Strangers. People who lived half a world away.

Zoe's face was radiant. Yet for Julie, the warm atmosphere of the club, the plush chairs encircling the cocktail tables, and the clusters of people squeezed in so close together that strangers were forced to become friends was hauntingly familiar.

Julie reached for her glass of Chardonnay, hoping that one more sip would quiet the panic that had suddenly, unequivocally taken her emotions hostage. She had to get out of there. Get away. Away from the encroaching feeling that she had lived such a moment once before. Portrait of a different place. Memories from a different time.

9

San Antonio, Texas
December 1974

A crystal ball hung high above the dance floor, casting prisms off the walls of the dimly lit room. Plush red Victorian furniture and round faux-marble-topped cocktail tables filled the dark corners of the small club.

Six months had passed since Mark Jennings had proposed on bended knee in front of the entire restaurant at The Stagecoach Inn. The customers had erupted in applause after I let out an exuberant, "Of course I will!" Mark had picked me up and twirled me around, sending the soft white strings of lights blurring into a dizzying euphoria.

The months had flown by and our wedding was now only seven days away. Between Mark's groomsmen and my bridesmaids, the wedding party practically represented a third of the states from the U.S., and as of last night, occupied the entire fifth floor of the local St. Anthony Hotel. My four bridesmaids had planned a pre-wedding bash at The Magic Time Machine, a place known for its groovy bands and wicked drinks. We were going to kick off a week of celebrating, and if any one group of people knew how to cut loose, it was certainly this one. Straining our eyes in the darkened room, Mark and I weaved our way amongst the tipsy crowd as "So Glad We Made It" reverberated loudly off the disco walls.

"Well, it's about time!" someone yelled from the back of the room.

"They'll just let anybody in here!" another voice chimed in, sparking a chorus of laughter audible above the pulse and thump of the band.

"Hey, this sounds like a rowdy group; could you use two more?" Mark taunted as the rectangular table of familiar faces came into focus.

Everyone had made it. Between Mark's Navy buddies and my attendants, the decision to jump-start the party without the guests of honor had apparently been an easy one. Sue had somehow managed to situate herself right next to Hank. Hank, Mark's friend with a body-builder physique, didn't seem to mind the unabashed attention Sue was shamelessly throwing his way. When I shot her a "you're sure not wasting any time look," she responded with a wink and edged even closer to him, sliding a whiskey sour across the table. "Let's toast everyone!" she said, holding her half-empty glass high in the air. "Here's to the happy couple!" She leaned closer in a botched attempt at a whisper. "And cute Navy guys."

"Here, here," I said, stifling a laugh.

The band played one popular hit after another. At the opposite end of the table, Sue had managed to pry herself away from Hank long enough to confer with Betsy and Renee about something. Their heads were pressed together and their hands covered their mouths. A mischievous plan was in the making.

"Wonder what kind of trouble they're brewing," I asked Mark with a nod in Sue, Betsy, and Renee's direction.

"Who knows with those three?" he said flippantly before downing another shot of tequila with the worm floating at the bottom.

A moment later Sue pushed back her chair, flashing a sarcastic look of mock defiance in my direction, stood up, flipped her long brunette hair over her shoulders, smoothed her skirt, walked in the direction of the stage, and slipped one of the band members a piece of paper.

"Come on!" Sue yelled as she grabbed my hand, dragging me to the microphone. "They're going to play our song!"

"*Wild thing, I think I love you,*" Betsy belted out, horribly off key, as she pulled her mic closer.

All five of us joined in singing, arms interlinked, heads moving with the beat, hips gyrating from side to side. The whole place erupted in laughter. We were either a huge hit or unknowingly humiliating ourselves. Either way, we were having the time of our lives.

I slid back into my chair next to Mark, exhausted from our dazzling attempt to entertain all the customers at The Magic Time Machine. Playfully nudging his shoulder, I asked him how we had done.

Without warning, Mark's expression morphed right in front of me. It was the first time I had ever seen such anger in anyone's eyes, much less the person I was about to marry in one week. Out of nowhere, the sting from the force of his hand slapping my face left me in a daze.

Our table, which moments before had exploded with laughter at one of Hank's corny jokes, was plunged into a sudden, unsettling quiet. Touching my cheek, I stared at him in total disbelief. As hard as I tried, words completely escaped me. Regret immediately flooded Mark's eyes.

"Baby, I'm sorry," he stammered.

I snatched up my purse and fumbled to the ladies room where I remembered seeing a payphone earlier that evening. I fought back an avalanche of emotions as my shaking fingers dialed the numbers. Standing outside in the freezing cold and gazing at the sleet through tear-stained eyes, I waited for my dad to pick me up.

Within minutes, the headlights of his white Buick Regal appeared in the darkness as he pulled into the circular drive. He didn't say a word on the way home. I knew that when I was ready to talk, he would be there to listen. But right then the quiet strength of his presence was more comforting than any words he could offer. We sat in silence, listening to the swish-swash of the wind-shield wipers sweeping away the sleet.

As our car turned onto the oak-lined street of my childhood home, I felt a small measure of relief at the tidy row of familiar houses. Daddy had taught Amy and I how to ride our first bicycles down the gentle slope just past our block. And the towering cypress tree in front of Chuck Williams' home had witnessed my very first kiss during a game of spin-the-bottle. A fleeting kiss, part of an adolescent's dream. Evenings spent chasing fireflies with empty Mason jars, and sleeping outdoors on an old Army cot, under a blanket of stars.

The Lone Star Ice House was still the local hot-spot where Debbie, Amy, and I had perched ourselves on red vinyl stools all those hot summer afternoons when a black cow and "Johnny Angel" crooning from the jukebox were as close to heaven as one could get. And it was here that I had succumbed to my first bad-boy crush. Andy, "the hood," with his dark, brooding manner, coal black hair, the brown comb protruding conspicuously from his back pocket, and cigarettes (real ones) stuffed in his front, had me thinking all kinds of thoughts. Thoughts that, had I been born Catholic like Debbie my neighbor, would have surely sent me scrambling to confession.

Now, I longed for those innocent, childhood days where my biggest worry was whether Chuck, Debbie, Amy, and I could pool enough money together to buy a single treat from the ice-cream truck. We were all in hog heaven as we split the Dreamsicle four ways.

As we pulled into the driveway, the familiar soft glow of the lamp in the window was soothing, a luminous bulwark against the freezing temperatures outside. Mom met me at the door and just held me. She had always been my safe place to fall, and the tears I had managed to stifle up to this point now freely flowed. I sobbed uncontrollably. Though I needed to, I still wasn't able to talk about the events of that evening.

"I'm sorry, Mom. We just had an argument, that's all," I whispered.

"I know, Jules...I know." Her hand gently wiped the tears from my face before I slid past her.

Within minutes, Mark was standing at the front door, begging me to come outside and talk to him. I didn't move...I just listened as I heard him pleading with my dad for a chance to see me.

For the first time in my life, my dad intervened.

"She'll call you tomorrow, Mark. Things'll look brighter in the morning. They always do." I'd heard the same speech dozens of times in high school, when I'd overreacted about some two-cent teenage drama. However, his uncharacteristically terse tone made me wonder if Daddy suspected more than I was telling.

The muffled shuffling of Mark's labored footsteps grew fainter. His car door slammed and I buried my head deeper into the pillow that was by now soaked from my tears. Gravel crunched underneath the tires of his Firebird as he backed out of the driveway, and the headlights sliced through the curtains of my window like a knife as the car stopped for a moment. My breath caught in my throat. It was as if he was letting me know he was there, one last desperate attempt to try and connect with me somehow. And then the shadows filled my room once again as his car turned onto the street, retreating into the darkness.

That night I tossed and turned, listening to the cold wind make an eerie sound as the tree limbs scratched against the windows. I cried until my eyes became heavy, drained from the emotions, and mercifully, just before dawn, sleep finally came.

My parents did not wake me the following morning, but the ringing of the phone in the hallway did. As I slowly tried to open my eyes, I found that they were swollen almost shut. I blinked, trying to convince myself to get up. The sunlight burst into the room, unwelcome. I heard my dad answer the phone.

"She's still asleep, Mark, but I'll tell her you called."

The door creaked as my dad poked his head inside. "You awake yet, sunshine?" he asked softly.

Daddy hadn't called me that in years, but his affectionate nickname made me feel like a twelve-year-old child again.

"Mark called. But before you call him back, your mother's made your favorite breakfast. Why don't you wash up and join us."

Staring at the two eggs accompanied by a link of Jimmy Dean sausage, too upset to eat, I once again contemplated my role in what had happened the night before and what could have possibly caused such extreme anger. I couldn't understand how he could get so mad at something so innocent.

Daddy sounded like he was a million miles away when he said, "Your mother and I want you to know that every relationship has its ups and downs, Jules. And weddings always add a lot of stress. We don't know what happened; just know that we'll support you no matter what."

"Thanks, Daddy. I guess I'd better call Mark back." Suddenly, I had an urge to hear what he had to say. Hoping desperately for an apology and some sort of rational explanation.

I stood up and Mom's hand gently covered mine as I reached for my plate. She looked in my eyes, the way she had done countless times when I was a teenager and she didn't think I was really listening, "Jules, we're here when you're ready to talk."

"I know, Mom."

I placed the dishes in the sink, ran some water over them, and took one last sip of orange juice. Staring out the back window, I watched as the sunlight bounced off of Mom's mirrored chimes hanging from the oak tree, scattering prisms about the patio. I leaned down and gently kissed her on the cheek. "Thanks for making the breakfast. It was delicious."

On my way to call Mark, I saw his blue Firebird pulling up into the driveway. My heart caught in my throat. Stepping out of the car, he looked up at the house, slowly shutting the door behind him as though trying not to make a sound. The confident man I was engaged to now looked more like a whipped puppy, and I found myself almost feeling sorry for him.

He looked bad. I'd never before seen him with bags under his bloodshot eyes. Dark and sunken. His shoulders slightly hunched over, hands shoved meekly in the pockets of his jeans as he fumbled up the short sidewalk. An inner battle was being waged. I should have been mad. Furious. A woman looking for some retribution, but those feelings simply weren't there. I wanted to scoop *him* up and tell him it would all be okay. Tell him what I knew he had come over to hear. But I couldn't. Not yet. The icy cold ground against

K. C. HARDY

my bare feet didn't even faze me as we stood there in silence.

"Julie," he said, reaching for my hand. "I'm sorry. I don't know what came over me. I shouldn't have gotten so angry." His head hung down in shame. There was no likeness to the Mark I knew, but right now it was what I needed to see. Remorse. "I didn't mean to hurt you, I'd never do that. Can you forgive me?"

I paused, letting his words hang in the frigid air. Unsure of what to say.

"But *why*, Mark?" I finally asked, blurting out the words, realizing he still hadn't really given an answer. "*Why* did you do it?"

He looked away and shrugged his shoulders.

"I don't know, Jules. I guess I just got jealous."

"You *guess* you just got jealous? Jealous of *what*?"

"All the guys, the way they looked at you up there. It drove me crazy."

"I couldn't help that!" I said incredulously.

"I know, I know Jules," he stammered, shaking his head before looking down at his shoes. "I'll never get that angry again. If I have to spend the rest of my life proving that to you I will."

The chilling December air cut straight to the bone. It was the kind of cold that not even a pair of sweatpants and an oversized sweatshirt could deter. But standing there looking at him struggling to find the right words, the hurt seemed to melt away.

Church was the last place I wanted to be the next morning. My self-pity far outweighed the desire to sing hymns of praise and worship. But my parents had insisted, a rare phenomenon since they believed strongly in non-interference. The pastor's message on forgiveness was a particularly poignant one and I felt as though it was directed specifically at me.

Forgiveness. A cornerstone of the Christian faith. A virtue you were supposed to bestow lavishly even upon your enemies. A lesson my parents had instilled in me from the time Mary-Ellen, our next-door neighbor and close friend, had not invited me to her sixth birthday party.

The divine message had been received. Not that I wouldn't have come to the same conclusion on my own, in my own time. But my pastor's words helped my foregone conclusion. So, once again, I regained the excitement that fewer than forty-eight hours earlier had been snatched out from underneath me. For my own sake, sitting there in the fifth pew of Oakdale Methodist Church that December morning, I convinced myself that I did believe him, and I could forgive him...after all, what choice did I have? I was head over heels for Mark Jennings.

10

San Antonio, Texas
December 18, 1974

ecember 18 snuck up on everyone. Two days before our wedding. For the past five days, I had been scurrying about like every bride does amidst the onslaught of last-minute thoughts that invariably crop up before a wedding. Six months of planning, appointments, and endless checklists, all to ensure that for five hours, everything that possibly could go wrong—didn't.

The day had started at the crack of dawn with breakfast at Apple Annie's Café in Boerne, a sleepy little town just north of San Antonio. The happy morning special complete with two eggs over easy, two slices of bacon, and a cup of Folgers were the perfect remedy for my already-growling stomach. The café, with its wall-to-wall frames that chronicled the history of the little town, worn-out vinyl booths that caved slightly under the weight of its customers, and the waitresses who knew all the secrets this town had to hold, had been a Saturday morning staple for our family as long as I could remember. Classic country hits boomed through the speakers of the juke-box in the corner, and the flickering rainbow bulbs on the Christmas tree in the window shone with a tranquil joy. With a coffee pot in hand, Judith bustled over, clad in her blue and white checkered apron, black ball-point pen jutting from her mound of fiery red curls. Her wiry frame contrasted with her gravelly voice, hinting at her younger and wilder years. "Julie, hon, isn't that weddin' of yours this weekend?" she asked.

She always somehow managed to ask a question just as I was taking a bite. I quickly gulped down the eggs before replying, "Yes, ma'am."

"Well, you certainly got yourself a looker!" she said with an affectionate pat on Mark's shoulder and a not-so-subtle wink in my direction before sauntering back to the kitchen. Judith was also the town flirt.

Mark just looked at me, laughed, and shook his head. The Texas charm and small town ways amused him. He reached across the table for the salt and pepper. "You

sure we can't just elope?" he asked with that look that almost always led to him getting his way.

"I wish!" I laughed.

The crooked clock on the wall, which always looked
as though the next customer walking through the door
would knock it from its precarious position, indicated
that his parents would be touching down in less than half
an hour. "We better get a move on if we want to pick your
family up."

⸺ ⸺

We stood at the terminal, anxious for their arrival. Amy
had insisted on joining us. This was the moment when
the wheels of the wedding would be permanently set in
motion. The night before, my mother and I had dropped
off some welcome baskets to the St. Anthony Hotel.
Everything from bluebonnet seeds to pralines spilled
over the sides of the Texas-themed gift baskets. The itinerary was sandwiched somewhere in the middle, detail-
ing our plans to visit the Alamo as well as a brief trip to
Austin to see the Capitol—time permitting.

But as his parents exited the plane, it was apparent
that our plans would be changing. Mark glanced over
at me, his face contorted in shock. His father, now in a
wheelchair, was being pushed by one of the flight attendants down the tarmac, his mom following close behind.
The person I had met less than two years earlier was gone,

replaced by a frail, gaunt shell of a man who looked twice his age. His mother hadn't given us a clue. Reaching for Mark's hand, I gave it a squeeze.

The trip must have taken a lot of courage and will-power, a selfless act of love for his son. Mark hugged his parents while I welcomed the rest of his family. There was a somberness that everyone disguised with smiles and light-hearted conversation. Taking their cue, I would try to carry on the rest of the weekend as though everything *was* normal.

— ~

December 20, 1974, the day I'd dreamed about, was finally here. As soon as the photographer had snapped all the pictures of the girls, Amy and I slipped away from the wedding party to catch a peek inside the chapel.

"Oh Jules, it's beautiful!" Amy said, wide-eyed and peeking at the decorations through the cracked chapel doors. Red poinsettias, baskets of white lilies, and roses and candles adorned the altar.

Then, turning to me, she asked, "Remember all those weddings we put Barbie and Ken through?"

I laughed, recalling the make-shift shoebox adorned with lace and sticks that had sufficed as an altar. The laughter felt good and calmed my nerves.

Finally, the moment had arrived. As the chapel doors opened for our grandmothers to walk down the aisle, the soloist began to sing "Follow Me" by John Denver, its melody filtering down through the speakers and filling the chapel like an angelic voice from heaven.

> *Follow me where I go, what I do and who I know, make it part of you to be a part of me. Follow me up and down all the way and all around, take my hand and say you'll follow me.*

My heart was racing at break-neck speed. There was no turning back. But I didn't want to turn back. Mark had picked out the song. I would be following him halfway across the country, leaving behind everyone and everything that I had ever known and loved. But life without him simply no longer existed. He had me completely. Intricately. My future interwoven with his.

One by one the girls filed out of the choir room, their elegant green dresses swishing with every step. They looked beautiful.

My first choice had been red, but Renee, with her auburn hair, had emerged from the dressing room at the bridal boutique three months earlier with a look of trepidation and panic on her face.

"Jules, I know you love red. And I know the wedding is around Christmastime. But seriously? *This* does *not* go with my hair," she'd said with both index fingers pointing at the dress as though she had just discovered some eight-legged creature stowed away inside the mass of red tulle. "I look hideous." The moment had conjured up an immediate flashback to our eighth-grade sock-hop and the elaborately detailed bunny socks her mother had painstakingly made for the occasion. I had pitied my friend as we both sat in the back of her mom's '62 Cutlass on the way to the dance, a sullen look shadowing her normally happy face. It was obvious that she would have rather been caught in nothing but her underwear than be seen in those floppy-eared, pom-pom cotton-heel socks.

"Okay, point taken," I laughed.

And that was why we'd settled on green dresses. Amy looked radiant, so grown up. I guess until that moment, I hadn't realized my kid sister was no longer a little girl. She stood there poised and ready for the cue to start her measured stroll down the aisle. The pearl and rhinestone necklaces and earrings I had given the girls at the rehearsal dinner now sparkled with the slightest movement. Each girl carried a bouquet of red roses tied together with a red satin ribbon. Jenny, my cousin from Tennessee, caught my gaze and winked at me as if to say, I can't believe you're actually getting married. I smiled back, my heart pounding furiously as I waited for my turn.

The ring bearers and flower girls' wide eyes and nervous glances threatened of a major meltdown. I held my breath as they timidly started down the aisle past the hundred pairs of eyes gazing back at them adoringly. The flower girl was my godchild and the ring bearer was her five-year-old brother. I was confident they would rise to the occasion. And they did.

"You ready, sunshine?" My dad greeted me in the foyer with a huge smile.

"Daddy, I'm so nervous." My hands were shaking, and no matter how hard I tried to keep them steady, I was convinced that everyone noticed.

"Well, you certainly look gorgeous, no one can tell," he whispered back, giving me an affectionate, reassuring smile as he gripped my hand a little tighter.

Mom looked absolutely resplendent in an emerald green floor-length gown that brilliantly matched her eyes that were clear as glass, which, according to my dad, had snagged him hook, line, and sinker all those years ago. Eyes that were now misty as she gave me one final hug before it was her turn to walk down the aisle escorted by Hank. Ensign Hank Wallace looked even taller that day standing next to my mom, and kinder still as he tenderly patted her hand, sensing her anxiety about giving her older daughter away.

Looping my right arm through my father's left while clutching my bouquet of white roses and lilies, we started down the aisle to the tune of the pipe organ playing the traditional "Here Comes the Bride." The sweet smell of roses filled the church and I tightened the grip on my dad's arm. Whatever leftover fears that lingered from the incident at

The Magic Time Machine were immediately erased with a single glimpse of Mark waiting for me at the altar.

We had decided to write at least some of our vows ourselves, to include our moving to a new state to begin our life together. Sniffles could be heard around the small chapel. As the chaplain asked Mark if he took this woman to be his lawfully wedded wife, he said, "You bet I do," and the whole church burst into laughter.

After exchanging our vows, the lights dimmed and we lit the unity candle as two of my close friends from Austin sang "The Wedding Song." There was no doubt in my mind that I had made the right decision.

Then, all the formality went out the window when Pastor Michaels burst into a grin and proclaimed, "I now present to you Ensign and Mrs. Mark Jennings. Mark, you can finally kiss your bride!"

The church erupted in applause and whistles as we walked down the aisle for the first time as husband and wife. I had never been happier.

The bells were ringing as the church doors flew open. To my surprise, Mark had arranged for the groomsmen and other fellow officers to form the Arch of the Sabers. Together we walked under each one. The groomsmen looked so handsome in their Navy dress black uniforms. Keeping with tradition, the last two swords were lowered right before we reached them. Mark passionately kissed me to the delight of all our guests.

We planned to spend our honeymoon at a romantic resort on Lake LBJ, Texas. He had to report to Miramar in less than two weeks, which didn't leave us much time. But the truth was, it didn't matter where we were.

━ ～

"Good choice, Jules," he said as we pulled up in front of the condos nestled underneath the canopy of towering pecan and cypress trees. The smoky scent of a lit fireplace wafted through the chilly evening, warming up the senses. The nippy air propelled me forward at a faster pace, toward 3E, the building closest to the water but farthest from the parking lot. Vaulted ceilings lined with pine beams extended toward the sky, lending an airy, open feel to the confined quarters. The room was warm and rugged, the smells exotic, the atmosphere taut with anticipation.

Dark-framed pictures of sailboats and snapshots of fishermen proudly showing off their prize catch hung in perfect symmetry around the 800-square-foot lakefront condo. We had spent countless childhood vacations along the rocky shores of Lake LBJ. Every summer my mom's side of the family would make the fifteen-hour trip from Tennessee for our annual get-together. Growing up, I had counted down with excited anticipation the days until that time in July when for two glorious weeks, I would get to see my cousins once again.

Lazy days that had passed with swimming, tubing, and boating under the hot Texas sun. Steamy nights camped around the bonfire. Jenny, Ken, Amy and I roasting marshmallows to make s'mores, letting the chocolate drizzle from our mouths while our parents snuck in a round of gin rummy. Eight years had passed since those idyllic summer vacations, but I was hoping that the condos would be just as magical as I remembered.

While Mark unloaded the luggage, I scurried to find matches for the candles I had packed at the last minute. There was no junk drawer in the kitchen. No random box filled with the peripheral staples needed from time to time. The condo contained strictly the bare essentials. I was scolding myself for not having the forethought to pack them as well when I spotted an old box of matches on the fireplace mantle.

Flipping off the overhead lights and turning on the radio was all that was needed for romance to ignite the darkened space of our candlelit rental.

"Brrrr...it's really cold out there! Well, this is it," Mark exclaimed triumphantly as he tossed the last bag in the hallway, simultaneously reaching back with his foot, slamming the door and shutting out the cold in one swift motion. "Wow, Jules! This is nice." He looked around the living room, shaking his head in disbelief. As I breezed past him to light the last candle, a hint of Chanel no. 5 lingered in the air. "And you smell even nicer," he said, pulling me close.

The four little candles had magically transformed the sparse, rustic condo into an enchanting, romantic retreat. Without the glare of artificial light, the floor-to-ceiling windows that encompassed the lake-facing wall now twinkled like stars from the reflections of the cobalt blue flames.

Mark threw himself on the bed, resting his head on one shoulder. "You think you're gonna get lucky or somethin', Whitaker?" He flashed a teasing grin, reaching for the celebratory bottle of champagne sitting on the nightstand, a sinful smile dancing in his eyes.

"I already am lucky. And that's Jennings to *you*," I reprimanded playfully, tapping the tip of his nose, my mouth curling up ever so slightly.

"Yes, ma'am. I'll take orders from you any old time." He saluted as his husky voice trailed off. He effortlessly pushed the champagne cork with his thumb sending it flying across the room. Then, pouring us each a glass, he raised his in the air: "To new beginnings."

"To San Diego." I said, holding my glass up to his.

Tonight there was a determined look in his eye. He knew what he wanted. I knew what he wanted. What he had been longing for since that first night after the Navy Ball. Over the past two years he had been the proverbial "officer and a gentleman," always hinting for more, but settling for less... much less. But now there was no more waiting. No more settling. His athletic body, normally so tough and hurried, was now still and patient. His slow kisses, now free of all constraints and moral servitude. Passion that could no longer be contained. He hovered over me, pulling me even closer. I ran my hands along his muscled back. The candles and sparks from the embers in the stone fireplace provided the only light in the room. The sensation of his lips against my skin sent chills up and down my spine. My heart pounded furiously in my chest.

He tenderly swept away the hair from my shoulders and kissed my neck. His hot breath felt like electricity.

"You know I've been waiting for you all my life," Mark whispered.

"Was I worth the wait?" I asked.

"Were you worth the wait? Hmmm...I'll have to check back later with you on that one," he laughed.

I swatted his arm. "I'm serious!"

"So am I." He laughed again. That hearty laugh that always gave me a glimpse into what he must have been like as a child. Then his face became solemn, his voice soft. "You were definitely worth the wait, Mrs. Jennings," he whispered, tilting my face up to his.

I smiled. The reflection of the fire flushed his face, and I knew that this image of Mark and this perfect moment would never leave me.

11

San Antonio, Texas
Christmas 1974

After the brief honeymoon, Mark and I returned back to my apartment to finish packing for San Diego. Moving always gave me a headache, something I first discovered freshman year when I had packed up my dorm for the summer to head home. I had been amazed to find how much was actually crammed into the eleven-by-fourteen rectangular room. A fact that had not been lost on my dad, who had generously taken off work, arriving that morning to help.

"Goodness gracious, Julie Elizabeth! You didn't have a tenth of this stuff in the fall. Where on earth did *all this* come from?" he had asked as he picked up the fourth box in a row that had "Julie's clothes" scrawled haphazardly in black Sharpie.

I swore at the time that I hadn't done *that* much shopping. But the "proof was in the puddin'" as my pappy would have put it. This time was no different. As my headache started pounding with a greater sense of urgency, I searched for the bottle of Vanquish that had long ago been tucked inside the box marked "bathroom."

"Quitting so soon?" Mark paused, brushing a trickle of sweat away with the back of his hand that also gripped a Phillips screwdriver. It was almost Christmas, but South Texas had been hit with a warm-front two days earlier, replacing the welcome winter blast with this shorts-and-t-shirt weather that Mark just loved, and I loathed. Funny, no matter where you are from, you're sure you were meant to be born somewhere else. A fact that had irritated my grandmother every winter when the Rio Grande Valley was flooded with "those *darn* snowbirds flying south. All parking their RVs along Highway 83 like they were all high-falutin' or something." Looking back, I think the root of it lay in a deep-seated resentment after being yanked out of her beloved Arkansas, and dropped off in this "devil's den," as she so often liked to describe the Valley. She was strong though, and she'd made the best of it, and I think that somewhere along the way she'd secretly grown to like it.

She and Pappy's smiling faces stared back at me from the wooden frame on the bookshelf. The picture had been taken on Pappy's eightieth birthday right after he had blown out his eight candles (one for every decade). His eyes glistening behind those deep wrinkles underneath that old dusty hat I'd never seen him without. A lone groove in the floorboard was the only testament to all those summers he'd spent rocking in those khaki suspender overalls on their front porch, talking away the world's troubles with Mamaw. I could almost smell the sweet, smoky aroma of his pipe sifting through the warm, coastal breeze that made my normally straight-as-an-arrow hair instantly frizzy. Tucked in the corner of the frame was a wallet-sized photo of me donning nothing more than bloomers and a smile while sitting on top of a watermelon that was bigger than I was. Pappy and I had just returned from delivering a truckload of watermelons to Luling, keeping one to share with the family. I'd found the old picture in the back room of their small white wooden pier-and-beam home the day after we had buried Mamaw. The room where as a child, she used to lie next to me at night weaving wonderful tales of far-away lands and beautiful princesses. White lace curtains floating in the summer breeze as the cicadas and crickets performed their nighttime symphony. Pappy had passed away two years prior, and there had been so much to go through for my dad and me. They were both gone now, and we'd had an awful time trying to pack away a lifetime of memories.

"Earth to Jules!" Mark said loudly.

"Huh?"

"I've called your name three times! What's going on inside that pretty head of yours? You still lookin' for that bottle of Vanquish?

"Yep," I said, putting down the picture and continuing on with my forgotten search.

"I could have gone to the Piggly Wiggly for you and been back by now. You want me to throw this in the trash?" he asked, holding up a life-sized poster of the UT tower taken the night we'd won the national championship.

He chuckled at the look of horror on my face as I retorted, "Are you crazy, Jennings?"

"I know, I know," he said turning back to the bed. "Just wanted to snap you out of your fog."

"How's it going with the bed?" I asked.

"Piece of cake!" he said.

He turned up the radio and went back to work dismantling the headboard from the bed-frame so he'd be ready when Daddy came to load it onto the truck. Elton John's "Mona Lisas and Mad Hatters" reverberated off the blank walls and bare floors, his clear soulful voice serenading us with the new hit that had sent me scrambling to buy his latest album, *Honkey Chateau*. "*You stand at the edge while people run you through; and I thank the Lord there's people out there like you*," I sang along. Mark dragged the footboard across the room and leaned it against the wall. He crept up behind me, grabbed my hand, and twirled me around.

"Maybe a little dance will help chase that headache away," he said.

"I doubt it," I moaned, feeling guilty for letting that darn headache get the best of me. It was Christmas time after all. Our first Christmas as husband and wife. Calling Mark my husband would take some getting used to. But the word alone made me flutter inside with pride. He was all mine! I leaned against him, swaying as Elton John serenaded us and rested my head on his chest.

We had arrived home late the night before from Lake LBJ, stretching out the honeymoon as long as possible, relishing every last dying ember from the fireplace—a classic avoidance technique for the inevitable chaotic days that lay ahead. The next week would be a frenzy of activity and impossible to-do lists. Christmas was in five days. And we were also busy packing for the move to San Diego, home of Miramar Naval Air Station, where Mark was scheduled to begin the Top Gun program. With the excitement of the wedding, I hadn't even finished my Christmas shopping. Truth be told, I hadn't even started. But now, as the last chord of "Mona Lisas and Mad Hatters" dropped off, the thought was thrust front and center and I reluctantly returned to the task at hand. My parents would understand. But it was the idea of shopping for my new in-laws that was no doubt fueling my headache.

The phone rang in the kitchen.

"I'll get it!" I hollered, clamoring over boxes and clumps of crumpled newspaper to reach the yellow phone anchored on the wall.

"Julie?" a feeble voice asked.

"Yes, this is she," I responded, swiftly changing my tone from one of mild annoyance to concern.

"It's Bev, hon. Is Mark there?" she asked.

"Yeah, sure. Just a sec," I said.

Mark had moved on from dismantling the bed and was placing another box on top of the two dozen already stacked by the front door.

"It's your mom," I mouthed, covering the receiver with my hand when he looked up at me.

Wiping his hands on his jeans, he took the phone. "Hey, Mom. What's up?" His face dropped as he listened, not once interjecting a question, not even saying a word. His forehead creased. His body slumped against the counter. He took the phone into the dining room, stretching the cord even further, forcing the spirals into a straight line. "So, what are they gonna do now?" he asked, followed a few minutes later by a deflated, "Oh..."

His hand nervously combed over the back of his head. He paced back and forth, his work boots scuffing the floor. He hung up, then picked up the receiver and slammed it down again.

Mark didn't look at me as he leaned his head back against the cupboard, staring up at some invisible spot on the ceiling, and said, "They had to stop the chemo, Jules. Dad's only been given a few weeks to live."

I walked across the room and wrapped my arms around him, holding him as tightly as I could. "I'm so sorry, babe."

He didn't respond.

"We need to go back up there," I broke the silence.

"I know. But there's so much to do, Jules, and we need to be in San Diego right after Christmas."

"We'll get everything done. Let's just have the movers put our stuff in storage until we arrive."

That evening, with my parents and Amy's help, we feverishly finished packing and Mark and I booked the first flight the next morning for Virginia.

Arlington had received a foot of snow the week before. The way it blanketed the ground seemed to mirror the gravity of the situation. Unlike my first visit, this time there was no joking around, no off-key carefree duets to the Mamas and the Papas. This time, there was two hours of nothingness on the drive from the airport: eerie silence and the blank expanse of highway, and bleak landscape draped in the dreary color of an ashtray. I yearned to go back to the last time we had driven these highways together. To the happier, care-free days.

I reached over and squeezed his hand. He didn't squeeze back. We pulled up in front of the home, and Mark sat there staring at it as though seeing it for the first time. "Somehow it looks different, doesn't it?" he asked, exhaling slowly.

"The people you love are still inside," I said reassuringly, but feeling the same overwhelming sadness.

"Yeah. But it's changed—already. It's not the same," he said, shaking his head and biting his lip.

"I wish I could make it better, Mark."

"I'm just glad you're here," he said, gripping my hand tightly.

I suddenly flashed back to my last visit, to the moment right after we had pulled into the driveway when Carl tapped on the window, causing me to jump out of my skin. He was such a strong man, stoic in every sense of the word. Strength molded into every chiseled bone of his face. Nothing about Mr. Jennings was weak. And yet, I knew that somewhere inside that house, the patriarch of the family sat imprisoned in a wheelchair. A blanket supplying the warmth that his weakened body could no longer provide. Glancing at the quiet house while I pulled my luggage out from the back seat, I wondered if he had watched us arrive. If he had situated himself in front of one of the many windows that graced the front of the home simply for the chance to catch a glimpse of his son.

We stomped the snow off our boots in the mudroom and hung up our jackets and my scarf. The side door slammed shut behind us.

~ ~

Everyone pulled together to make this time as special as possible. A whirlwind of activity followed our arrival.

His mom emerged from the kitchen. "You're early, sweetheart. What a nice surprise!"

"Yeah, we were able to catch an earlier flight," Mark said, kissing his mother on the cheek.

Lori appeared from the living room, fresh ivory sheets rolled up in her arms. "Hey there. You're just in time to help Steve move the guest bed down here." She planted a brief peck on Mark's cheek.

"Boy, you don't let a man rest, Lori," Mark joked before tackling the stairs two at a time to the guestroom.

"Good to see you too, Julie," she said, offering up a tired smile.

"You too, Lori," I said, returning her smile with a hug. "Let me help you with those sheets once the boys get the bed down here."

"I'll take you up on that offer," she responded handing over the stack of ivory colored linens.

Over the next five days, in spite of the devastating prognosis, his dad tried hard to put on a brave front.

Steve and Lori stayed at the house for the entire week, and even JR removed his headphones long enough to emerge from his room for more than fifteen minutes.

On our first full day there, we all visited a local tree farm. The normal tradition was to let the kids pick out the perfect Christmas tree while Carl would saw it down. Normal, however, was nowhere in sight—vanished along with all the other traditions no one dared to mention.

This year, there wasn't even a whisper of normalcy. Not even in the rows and rows of Christmas trees that Mark and his family had visited every year since he was a child. This year, Mark pushed his dad around in the snow until he spotted a blue spruce worthy of being the Jennings' 1974 Christmas tree. The six-foot tree was majestic, and within minutes Mark had sawed clear through the eight-inch trunk.

Back home, JR and I steadied it in the stand while Steve and Lori snapped about orders from the couch to move the tree first this way, then that. And when we finally had it in the approved spot, Mark screwed in the fasteners to hold it in place. I thought about Mom, Dad and Amy, who I was certain by now had already picked out a much smaller tree this year from the Piggly Wiggly lot and placed it in front of the large picture window. Surely it had already been decked out in the same sparkly tinsel, bubble lights, and six-inch angel that had adorned it every Christmas for as long as I could remember. The Jennings' tradition felt like something out of a Norman Rockwell painting, I thought, while gingerly taking another sip from the piping hot cup of cocoa. Bing Crosby's "I'm Dreaming of a White Christmas" emanated from the stereo. The entire scene conjured up all those buttery sweet memories of home.

That night after decorating the blue spruce, we sat next to the crackling fireplace sipping on hot chocolate while Steve flipped through the channels on the T.V., settling on *It's a Wonderful Life*. Beyond the frosted window, past Beverly and Carl, a winter wonderland sparkled beneath the half-moon above. The tall, dark trees swayed in the chilly nighttime breeze. If someone were to take a snapshot of us sitting there—Lori asleep on Steve's lap on the floor, Beverly's head on Carl's shoulder, and me leaning back against Mark's chest—no one would have guessed the grueling tide that tugged underneath, the dark shadow that blunted our Christmas mirth. Each tick on the clock situated above the fireplace mantel stole what little time was left like a thief in the night. And sometime after Jimmy Stewart delivered his famous line, "Well, just come back here, mister. I'll give her a kiss that'll put hair back on your head," I fell asleep.

The following morning over coffee and bagels, Mark's brother suggested we all go tobogganing. We didn't have to go far. We retrieved the sleds from the garage and simply trekked across the street to the green belt that was composed of several rolling hills. I had never been sledding before. Aside from the occasional winter storms in Tennessee that happened to coincide with our annual visits, this was my first experience with this much snow.

"Gentlemen, start your engines!" JR teased, waving a bright red handkerchief that doubled as a racing flag. The boys playfully moved back and forth, threatening a false-start like they were racing in the Indy 500. I sat behind Mark, my arms clinched tightly around his waist, sure that the gritty competitor would be quick on the draw. I glanced over at Lori, who rolled her eyes in an exaggerated fashion at the boyish immaturity of our husbands.

"Come on, JR!" Mark laughed. "Stop swishing that thing around, and let us go."

"I'll tell you to go, when I'm good and ready!" he said.

"Will you just say it al—"

Steve didn't have a chance to finish his plea before JR defiantly, in a flash, lowered the flag and yelled, "Go, you *pansies*!"

As the sled picked up speed, I tightened my grip around Mark's waist. A cold blast of air hit our faces and we shrieked excitedly while flying downhill at lightning speed. Snow sprayed my face and pelted my dry eyes as my stomach did somersaults. As soon as our sled slowed to a stop, Mark jumped off, grabbed the sled along with my hand, and together we raced back up to the top to do it all over again.

For a brief moment in time, the veil of sorrow that draped heavily around us had lifted. And we were all children, once again.

12

Miramar NAS
San Diego, California
January 1975

Mark's parents and brothers drove us to the airport—his dad insisted on seeing us off at the gate. Carl normally would greet his son with a firm handshake and a pat on the back and would send him off in the same manner. This time, though, things were very different. When the ticket agent announced that Flight 372 bound for San Diego was boarding, I could see the conflicting emotions spread across

Mark's face as he strained to put up a brave front for his father.

"I'm proud of you, son," Mr. Jennings said, his eyes welling up with tears. "The Navy's lucky to have you. You're gonna make one heck of a pilot."

"Thanks Dad, that means a lot. Hell, if I'm anything like my old man, I'll be right up there with the best of 'em," Mark swallowed hard, bent down and embraced his dad in a tight hug, holding on as long as he could before standing back up and throwing his carry-on over his shoulder.

As Mark and I walked to the jetway, we turned around to wave a final goodbye to his parents. And what happened next would be the image that would be seared in my memory every time I thought of Mr. Jennings. Carl saluted his son, and held his hand at attention, his eyes somberly fixed on his son. Mark, clicked his heels, stood up straight as an arrow, slowly raised his hand to his forehead, and returned his father's salute. Struggling to keep his emotions in check, he stood frozen in that position for a few moments before taking my hand and turning to board the plane.

On the three-hour flight to San Diego, he was quiet. The light drizzle that fell on the tarmac as we touched down at the San Diego International Airport did little to lighten our spirits. We drove straight to Miramar Naval Air Station and the temporary base housing that would be our home until a more permanent one could be found.

Mark was scheduled to start training in three weeks. He would be a part of the Navy's Top Gun program, assembled from a carefully hand-picked group of elite pilots from across the nation. But first he was required to attend SERE school (short for Survival, Evasion, Resistance, and Escape) the following Monday. As we walked in the door and saw rooms of boxes waiting for us, we both collapsed from sheer exhaustion on the one thing that didn't need to be unpacked, the couch.

"Okay, Mrs. Jennings, you ready to break in your new house?" Mark said with a wink, his hand already reaching over to pull me closer. Obviously, no amount of personal pain could temper his desires. But, it might have been just what the doctor ordered. We were still newlyweds after all. "I've been waiting twelve hours to get my hands on you."

"Twelve *whole* hours?" I said in my exaggerated, Scarlett O'Hara, Southern damsel-in-distress voice, punching him playfully on the shoulder. "Oh, you poor thang!"

A loud knock on the front door jolted us.

"Jennings, you there?" a man's voice bellowed from the front porch.

"Shoot!" I said, hurriedly buttoning up my blouse.

Mark waited for me as I scampered to get dressed before he opened the front door. "Hey, Buckner," Mark said. "I didn't know you were already here." The two men shook hands.

"Karen and I got here last week, and we've already unpacked. She's at the store now though, getting things for dinner. Saw your car. You need a hand with anything?"

"Thanks, man, appreciate the offer. But we just got here and we're pretty beat. I think we're just going to crash and tackle everything tomorrow." He turned slightly toward me so that only I could see his sly smile.

In spite of the intermingling thoughts of his dad, and the occasional feelings of homesickness, Mark and I did our best over the next week to regain the spark from our honeymoon. However, early Sunday morning, only five days after we arrived in San Diego, Mark's mother called. His father had taken a turn for the worse.

Within three hours we were on the next flight to Arlington. Despite being fully aware of the bleakness of his father's situation, his mother's grim news came as a shock to both of us. Being the eternal optimist, I had stubbornly clung to hope that he would be able to defy the odds in spite of the doctor's grim prognosis. Once again, Mark was unusually quiet on that flight, and this time, I felt powerless to comfort him. I could only hope that we would get there in time. Mark seemed to be in his own world, a world in which I was suddenly not a part of.

Lori and Steve met us at the airport, but their laughter and smiling faces from last time were replaced with tears of anguish. We hadn't made it in time. His dad had passed away. Mark dropped his bags, staring blankly off into space, face taut. I could feel the emptiness...the despair.

As soon as we got to the house, he left to go with his brothers to the funeral home to make the final arrangements. Mark's dad had appointed him executor of his will. Shoulders that normally could carry the weight of the world now looked as if they would crumble with the slightest cross-wind. I stayed behind with his mom to keep her company while Lori ran to the store to get a few things. It was only my second experience with death, but my first as an adult, and as I went into the kitchen to fix her a pot of coffee, I groped blindly for words that might convey any sort of solace.

She sat down at the kitchen table where her Bible lay open to the Book of Matthew. I noticed a distinctive scent of lavender that trailed behind her. She pulled her pink terry-cloth robe even tighter around her. I talked about what a kind and wonderful man her husband was and that even though I had only known him for a short time, I too had grown to love him. She nodded, her finger mindlessly tracing the rim of her coffee cup as she stared blankly ahead.

The house that had been filled with so much laughter on each of our visits now sat depressingly quiet. Devoid of life. Still. The bubbling repetition of the percolator and the drone of the heater were now amplified in the somber silence. The heavy wooden chair scraped across the wooden floor as I pulled it out. The impeccably dressed woman now sat next to me, her soul as bare as her feet. Her blonde hair was left to its own devices, jumbled in a soft tousled mess on her shoulders while her smooth complexion, normally made over to debutante perfection, now revealed the few creases that hinted of the years behind them. And yet, she had a youthful radiance and an inner beauty that I had not noticed before. Most likely because I had been too consumed with her opinions of me, rather than how I felt about her. It was a vulnerable moment. Her grief exposed. And in that dark breakfast room, shades drawn at 505 Pleasant Valley Drive, I pulled my chair even closer.

At the funeral, we stood knee-deep in snow at the grave site, and for only the second time since I had known him, tears trickled down Mark's face as he stared at the flag-draped casket. The trees, dusted lightly with remnants of the snowfall from the day before, stripped of any leaves, shivered with us as I wrapped my black coat tighter still around me and stuffed my hands deeper into the wool pockets. About a third of the mourners from the church had joined the procession to the cemetery and now stood with us shoulder to shoulder as the pastor read from the twenty-third Psalm. A verse I had memorized as a child. Mark held a glassy stare that reached beyond the rows of white headstones, past the pastor who was now giving his interpretation of why King David referred to the Lord as his Shephard, as opposed to a litany of other titles he could have chosen, and into the vast expanse of the snowy terrain beyond. I felt helpless watching him suffer so much and felt so inadequate to help. Mrs. Jennings sat stoically as she watched the honor guard meticulously fold the flag of the nation her husband had proudly served. And as one of the servicemen kneeled and tenderly handed it to her, asking her to accept it on behalf of a grateful nation, a single tear ran down her cheek, dropping onto the flag now folded in her lap.

It seemed like just as quickly as we had arrived, we were boarding the plane, once again heading back to California. Mark was to report to the base early the next morning to begin his SERE training. He would be gone two weeks, and this without question was going to be the longest two weeks of my life. I was worried about him having to do this so soon after losing his father. He and his dad had always been so close. After all, he was the son who'd followed in his footsteps. Would all of this push him over the edge? I repressed the thought.

The two weeks Mark was away, I took the opportunity to get a little more acclimated to San Diego. Temporary base housing was different, but definitely had its perks. Everything was within walking distance, which was a very good thing considering I'd asked Daddy to sell my mustang. On a military budget, you vetoed fluff luxuries, so a second car was the first obvious exclusion. Daddy, true to form, was able to sell my car and mailed me the check.

Holding the check, I was reminded of the day Daddy helped me buy my first car. Responding to an ad in the paper, we drove an hour to find it on an abandoned old farm. Daddy had rolled up his sleeves, lifted the hood and checked out the engine. I remember thinking how handsome and remarkably young looking my dad still was. His toned arms lifted a few wires and caps and checked fluid levels. My friends in middle school had all had a crush on him. And although I feigned ignorance and slight disgust at why they thought *my dad* was so cute, I'd had to admit he bore a striking resemblance to Rock Hudson. And I was sure it was the reason he'd been picked to appear in a national commercial for his company. We'd all sat around the television in the den, waiting giddily for the ad to appear in a commercial break during an episode of *All in the Family*. Daddy, just shaking his head from his corner chair, had laughed at the absurdity of mom, Amy and I making such a fuss over his newfound fame. But for a year, every time that commercial aired, the three of us girls had felt a sense of pride that the handsome and yet humble man darting across the television screen was ours. After he was finished checking out the engine he'd shimmied underneath the car and given the undercarriage a once-over to see if it'd ever been involved in an accident. I remembered him driving home that day, since I didn't know how to drive a stick shift just yet. I'd quickly learned a week later in the vacant parking lot adjacent to the Dairy Queen. Daddy had been so patient in teaching me how to drive the four speed mustang —the car violently jerking as it lurched forward before sputtering to a stop—over and over and over again. It took half a day and about two dozen attempts to finally get the

K . C . H A R D Y

timing right of when to ease off the clutch, methodically pressing on the accelerator while shifting from zero to first. Now, standing here holding the check, I felt of tug of affection for my parents.

Our new home was small, an efficiency albeit, but the eight hundred square foot apartment was all that we needed. And I loved San Diego. The air smelled different here. A hint of ocean, entwined with flowers and sandy beaches. It reminded me of clothes freshly strung on a line, drying in the warmth of the sun. I loved being in walking distance to everything I needed from the Officers Club to the commissary. Everywhere I looked I was reminded of the fact that I was a California girl now, and the mild temperatures that always hovered just around perfect drove that feeling home even more. I loved the towels that were draped over balcony railings and how surfboards were visible on neighbor's patios. The group barbecues where anyone and everyone within close proximity knew they were invited...no invitation necessary. You just needed to bring something to contribute. Maybe it was San Diego or the fact that we were living in a military community, but everything had a cohesiveness that I loved. A sense of community drawn together by a common purpose. And although it was a base, aside from the continual roaring of fighter jets in training overhead, it felt far removed from the arduous reason it existed. Everyone was friendly and welcoming to newcomers. A collection of transplants from all over the country, most everyone removed from their family and friends, the bonds of friendship forming more quickly.

I placed several calls to Beverly both weeks that Mark was away at SERE school. I worried about her being alone in that big house. Worried about what it must have been like to have everyone home, converging on your house with a swell of laughter, tears and grief, and then just as quickly as they'd arrived, they'd left once again, leaving the home as empty as it had been before their arrival. Perhaps even emptier. Lonelier. Thankfully she still had JR, although his teenage mood swings and propensity to stay holed up in his room, headphones securely fastened to his ears probably didn't make for the most ideal companion during this time in her life.

During my calls, Beverly always let the conversation scale tilt more in my direction. She wanted to hear about what California was like. Did I like it? I told her I did, which was the truth. Had I heard from Mark? I told her I hadn't, but I was sure that he would get through it. Beverly's sister, Anna, had flown in to stay with her five days after the funeral. I felt better knowing someone was there to pre-occupy her. To hold the loneliness at bay for a few more days. Fill her with distractions from her grief. That's the beauty of family. I was confident Amy would have done the same thing for me. Amy. I missed her too. She'd promised to come and visit for a week over the summer. I was pretty sure the draw for her was more about California and its' white sandy beaches than me, but I was looking forward to her visit regardless of the motive.

I also took the opportunity to hang up some decorations and finish unpacking those few stubborn boxes that still lingered in the entry. We were still searching for a more permanent home close to San Diego, but it would never feel like home if we were constantly sifting through bags and boxes to find everyday staples.

Despite the distractions and lists, anxiety gnawed at me while Mark was away at SERE school. From what I had gathered from the other wives, the training was pure hell. The goal was to drag you down to the point of breaking your mind as well as your spirit. To survive torture, if you fell into enemy hands.

I'd begged Mark to see if he could postpone the training, fearing it was too much too soon. But the tough-guy persona didn't allow for weakness or grief. He would push through, persevere.

Mark returned home, as was expected, more subdued. Reticent. Reserved. But I didn't know whether to attribute it to grief, or SERE school. I guess it didn't matter, really. I just needed to be understanding and give him time to work through it. And so that's what I did. Wait for his cues. Give him the space he needed to sort through everything.

There was comfort in establishing a new routine. Our routine. The mornings were our time. The start of a new day unfolding over scrambled eggs, sizzling bacon, and toast smothered in butter and strawberry jam.

It took a few weeks, but slowly the Mark I knew started to re-emerge. Eight weeks after first arriving in California, we finally moved into our town home in Chula Vista, a quaint town outside of San Diego. The back of the townhouse faced the west so in the evenings we'd unwind on the back patio in the plastic fold-out lawn chairs and soak up the stunning California sunsets. That square concrete patio was our own blissful French Riviera. We planted a garden out back. We started jogging and taking long walks, and went swimming in the community pool on the weekends. We barbecued with our neighbors. Life was improving. Slowly becoming exactly how I had imagined it would be. And the seeds that we had planted in our small garden, were sprouting through the rich soil, reaching for the sun.

Trouble seemed to be lurking below the surface, however. A tremor undetectable by a seismograph, but waiting to explode nonetheless. Mark started having a night cap at the end of the day. It was usually only one, or two, occasionally followed by a third—after a particularly rough day. He'd sit in the lazy-boy watching *Mash*, laughing at the antics of the humorous characters. A distraction.

"Baby, come here," he'd say. Patting his lap. I willingly obliged. I loved being close to him. Nuzzling my face into his neck, letting his five o'clock shadow send tingles down my body. A hint of Bourbon smoothing away the rough edges of his day. The week. The month.

The happy go lucky man I had fallen in love with slowly started to reappear. But the other side, the morose side I'd first witnessed at the Magic Time Machine, started appearing more often as well. A switch triggered without warning. At times I couldn't predict. I found myself walking on pins and needles, catering to an invisible struggle where a war was being waged I couldn't see. Inner demons yet to be conquered.

He became increasingly agitated. Over stupid things. Like the time I forgot milk at the grocery store.

"Dammit, Jules. Can't you remember anything?" he'd snapped, snatching the keys from the hall table, slamming the front door before peeling out of the driveway.

Or the time John, April's husband, had offered me a ride home from the grocery store so I wouldn't have to walk home in the rain.

"You don't ride with other men, Julie," his voice had bellowed. "You call your husband."

"He was already there making a grocery run for April, Mark," I'd responded, bewildered at what the big deal was. "He offered. He lives four houses down!"

"That's not the point, Julie. You don't want to be giving off the wrong impression!"

"Okay, Mark. Whatever," I'd responded. I'd been conceding a lot lately—hoping to keep isolated situations from escalating.

But the good was still *so* good. Crazy good. When he wasn't angry he was the absolute best person in the world to be around. A man who could have a room in stitches, the life of the party. And in spite of all the rough times we had experienced over the past few months, my heart still melted when he walked through the front door at the end of the day. His love was an intoxicating cocktail I couldn't live without.

The third Saturday after he returned home, we planned on meeting some fellow pilots and their wives at the Officers Club for a night of dinner and dancing. We had eagerly anticipated a fun, relaxing evening all week. We both needed it...especially Mark. And the evening seemed to be headed in the right direction...

13

San Diego, California
Spring 1975

"Hey Mark, can I steal your wife for a dance?" Pete, another pilot and a friend of Mark's asked.

"Sure man. But you better keep your hands where I can see 'em!" he laughed, thrusting his drink in the air.

It wasn't the response I was hoping for. I had no desire whatsoever to dance with anyone else. But at Mark's repeated insistence, I followed Pete onto the wooden dance floor, glancing back at Mark with a puzzled look. By the time we got onto the floor, thankfully the song was almost over.

"Thanks, Pete," I said, hurriedly weaving my way back to the bar.

But he grabbed my hand and signaled to Mark that he wanted one more dance with me. With Mark's thumbs up, I was twirled around as the band started "You've Lost That Loving Feeling." The last thing I wanted to do was dance another slow song with Pete Anderson, but being rude was not an option.

When the song was over I wanted to leave, but Mark was adamant about staying. And although he acted as though everything was fine, going through his normal charade of joking with his buddies, with each bourbon and coke, his eyes began to reveal something else. A look that was hauntingly familiar. Leaning back against the bar on his elbows, he'd occasionally glance over at me when he thought no one else was looking. A cold, detached stare that conveyed everything. He took another sip of his stiff drink and cocked his head in my direction before lowering it once again, shaking it slowly in disgust. He chewed away on the black cocktail straw.

The band set down their guitars, taking a short break, and the opening chords to Sonny James, "Is it Wrong," came blaring from the brightly colored jukebox hiding in the corner, drawing a few couples onto the dance floor. I watched them for a few moments with more longing than jealousy. For five days I'd looked forward to this evening. Actually, more like a couple of months. Now, about ten songs and at last count four Bourbon and Cokes later, I was somberly coming to the realization that this was not going to be the night I'd envisioned.

"Well, if you don't want to leave, do you wanna dance?" I asked with a trace more desperation in my tone than I'd intended.

"Dance?" he scoffed. "You wanna dance?" He dropped his head back, meeting the glass to his lips, making sure to get every drop of the last swig. He slammed the glass down on the counter and slid it across to the bartender. A jerky nod indicated to fill it up. "Why don't you ask Pete?" he asked, looking me squarely in the eyes.

Mark was too busy fuming to notice that Pete was choreographing his next move with a busty brunette with feathered hair, heavy eyeliner and bright pink glossy lipstick. Her white peasant blouse with tasseled draw strings draped open just enough to lap up the attention she was seeking. *Where was 'tassels' when we first arrived?* I thought dryly. Pete always was a sucker for the ladies that screamed attention, and I was confident if that girl had been there when we'd arrived, Pete wouldn't have asked me to dance in the first place, and all of this could have been avoided.

"Pete's chatting it up with a Bridgitte Bardou lookalike," I said, hoping the sight would snap Mark out of his irrational thinking. Remind him that Pete was an eligible single bachelor who was always up for a good time. Not a man who was looking to steal his friend's wife. "Besides, I came to dance with my husband."

"Bull. That's a bunch of bull," he said motioning to the bartender that he'd changed his mind and was ready to close his tab. He swiveled around on the bar stool to face me. "If you wanted to dance with your husband, then why'd you dance with someone else."

His question was so ridiculous that I was momentarily caught off-guard. "You're the one who told me to dance with Pete! Why are you trying to turn this around on me?"

"I'm done," he said disgusted, slapping a twenty on the bar and pulling the keys out of his pocket.

Not a word was spoken during the ride home. I turned on the radio to quiet the intruding silence. Mark switched it off with such force that I was surprised the knob didn't break. Out of the corner of my eye I could see him swallow hard as he tightened his grip on the wheel. So rigid that his knuckles turned white. With a clenched jaw, he angrily focused straight ahead.

He finally spoke. "*Why*?" his voice raised, filled with angst.

"Why what?" I asked in complete bewilderment.

"Just answer my damn question."

"How can I answer a question you haven't even asked?" I shot back, my blue eyes flashing with annoyance.

"You know good and well what I'm talking about, Julie. Don't play dumb with me. You liked that. You really liked that, didn't you?" His words pierced the space between us.

"Liked *what*? Mark, what on earth are you talking about?" I asked again. "Let's discuss this in the morning. Please!"

"You liked dancing with Pete...I could see it in your eyes." His voice dripped with disdain—sarcasm oozing from every word. "You wanted to be with him."

I cast him an incredulous glance. He glowered back with an accusing eye.

"Oh, for crying out loud—I didn't even want him to touch me. *You're* the one who insisted I dance with him!" I said as we pulled into our driveway. By this time the decibel of my voice was so high I was certain that our neighbors could hear every word. I didn't care. I was enraged at the absurd accusation.

"Liar," he said, following me inside, the screen door slamming behind us, its metal hinges screeching. Then, without warning, he grabbed me by the arms and threw me on the ground, gripping me so tightly that the pain became excruciating. He hovered over me, his face red with rage. "You're a damn liar!" His words stung more than if he'd slapped me.

"Get off of me, Mark! You're just drunk." I tried to wrangle my way out of his tightening grip. "You're not thinking straight."

With malice, his hands reached for my neck. He hovered over me, eyes ablaze with rage, fingers squeezing around my neck like a noose. I tried prying his fingers away but was no match for him. Purple veins on his neck popped out. The pungent stench of bourbon on his hot breath suffocated me even more. Strong fingers clenched tighter. His arms locked into position like a hunter firing a final shot. My lungs seemed to be on fire as I struggled to catch my breath.

Suddenly he leaned back, slowly sinking into the floor. His head hung in uncharacteristic shame. His eyes closed. He took a deep breath and then clasped his hands behind his head. He didn't look up. His rapid breathing started slowing down. Coughing, I rolled over and curled into a ball, hoping to make myself invisible. Several minutes passed before he raised his head and still found me frozen in the same spot. "I'm sorry, baby, I'm so sorry."

Images from that night at the Magic Time Machine were thrust front and center. A sling-shot of emotions and memories rushed by like a violent roller coaster I couldn't get off. His cold gaze frozen with an unidentifiable fury, the sting of his hand on my cheek, the sleet that had been falling as I'd waited outside in the cold bitter air for daddy to pick me up. His answer to my question the following morning that at the time had seemed trite yet somewhat believable. An uncharacteristic, isolated, display of jealousy which would never happen again. Now all a lie. A promise—now broken.

Suddenly queasy, I garnered every ounce of strength I had and trudged up the stairs toward the bathroom, grasping the wooden rails to help steady my shaky legs. Locking the door, I lowered the lid on the toilet and sat down, burying my face in my hands, unable to stop the flow of tears. All the time wondering who we had just become.

Mark's steps approached the bathroom. He knocked softly. "Come on, Julie. Open up. I want to talk to you, baby."

He pulled again on the doorknob.

"Give me a few minutes, Mark."

The shadow of his shoes spilled underneath the door. I continued to hold my sides, rocking back and forth.

"Okay, Julie, this is enough," he said after several minutes.

Hesitantly, I unlocked the door.

"Baby, I'm so sorry. Nothing in this life scares me more than the thought of losing you." He buried his head on my shoulder.

"I know," was all I could manage to say. After all, how could I ever fully comprehend all that he had been through? It would just take time, I thought, trying to justify his actions and my decision once again to forgive. He's been through so much. But even as I repeated the familiar line of excuses in my head, I was beginning to question their validity.

— ⟡ —

The next couple of weeks I consciously pushed back the anxieties and concerns that now cropped up with more regularity. Over the past six months, I had developed an uncanny ability to deny the undeniable. For the most part, I was successful in pushing the events from that Saturday night at the Officer's Club out of my mind.

We settled into a natural rhythm complete with an early morning routine of breakfast with scrambled eggs and bacon or pancakes that I would prepare in what seemed like the middle of the night. It was an effort I made in hopes of narrowing the ever-widening gulf that expanded between us. We needed to talk...he needed to talk. But that was the one thing that couldn't be cooked up in those early hours before the rest of the world started their day. The time of the morning that is still black as coal, when not even a single bird is chirping. It was my hope, that in that quiet darkness and the peace that comes with a brand new day, we would somehow rediscover each other and find our way back. Our marriage was new, so fresh. And yet, we had already faced many trials—trials that would have tested even the most seasoned couples. Ever since the wedding, I couldn't help but feel that our young marriage was starting to spiral out of control. It seemed that our relationship had undergone a subtle but unmistakable shift and I wasn't sure if we would ever be able to return to the way we were before. And that, far beyond anything else, was my greatest fear. I worried about what Mark was not saying. What he was not showing. About him drinking more, and talking less.

Focusing on our problems day in and day out was not serving any purpose. I knew I needed something to occupy my time as well as my thoughts while Mark was at work. A doer by nature, idle hands did not sit well with me. Sitting alone hours on end in our townhome only magnified the events from the Magic Time Machine and

Officer's Club in my mind and fed my worst fears. My framed Texas nursing certificate still lay in one of the unpacked boxes in the hall closet. All I had to do was simply apply and pay for my California license, but this didn't seem like the right time to be taking on a full-time job. Adding another stress to an already tenuous situation.

During the two weeks that Mark was in SERE school I had become close with April, another navy wife and a teacher from New Jersey. At her suggestion, we decided to apply at the local Burger King. It would be an easy part-time job with hours that would still have us home for our husband's before they got off work. And to top it off, it was within walking distance. So, one Friday morning April and I walked to the Burger King and filled out an application.

The manager chuckled beneath his thick dark framed glasses when looking at our resumes, and said with a grin, "Welcome aboard and welcome to California."

If someone had told me four years earlier that after enduring countless all-nighters, suffering through days on end of sleep-deprived delirium in the campus library, that I'd be working at Burger King—much less actually liking it—I'd have certainly told them they were crazy. Out of their mind crazy. But here I was, donning my bright orange and yellow cap, pressing the button on the drive through intercom as I asked, "Would you like a hot apple pie to go with that Whopper, ma'am?" A question that always evoked a few giggles from my co-workers and exaggerated imitations of my Southern drawl.

Yet I was truly happy. It wasn't about the job. Or the extra income—contrary to what Mark thought. He didn't understand why I felt the need to work. He viewed the part-time, minimum-wage job as a slap in his face. An insinuation that he couldn't provide. What he couldn't understand, and what I didn't dare say, was that the walks to and from work in the cool afternoons with April were therapeutic. Relaxing. They made me miss Amy, Renee, and Sue a little less. And then there was Mr. Bradford, my manager. A big, burly guy whose quick wit and kind eyes reminded me of my dad's. He had a different joke to share at the start of every day while we were busy stuffing the napkin holders and re-filling the salt and pepper shakers. As awful as the jokes sometimes were, they always managed to make us laugh. And laughter was something that was in short supply at home these days. Burger King became a surrogate family to me. My only other connection to California, other than Mark and Wednesday's bingo night with the other wives.

"So, have you met your new neighbors two doors down?" April asked one afternoon while we were walking home from work.

"We have new neighbors?" I asked, shielding my eyes from the glare of the afternoon sun.

"Yes, we have new neighbors, silly! I can't believe you sometimes! They moved in a couple of days ago," she laughed. "The rumor is that they work at the Pink Cheetah around the corner," she continued.

"What in the world is the Pink Cheetah?"

"Jules," she shook her head in disbelief. "You pass by it at the turn-off to get to the base. You know the building with the blinking hot pink neon sign! There's absolutely *no way* you can miss that!"

"They're strippers?" I asked disbelievingly, recalling the sign she was talking about.

"Oh yah they're strippers! I've never seen a group of guys so eager to help someone move in! It was downright comical last Sunday, all of them lined up to help them carry in their furniture. According to John, their names are Candy and Cherry," she said trying to keep a straight face.

"Candy and Cherry?" I asked raising both eyebrows.

"Candy and Cherry." she said in a matter of fact tone.

"Hmm, well that explains a lot," I laughed, recalling our patio bar-be-cues and Mark's eager distracted glances toward the townhome two doors down. "I've seen them sunbathing all hours of the day and wondered if they worked. Mystery solved."

"Oh yah they work. They work hard for their money," she smirked as we both burst into laughter.

I loved walking home with April. Her funny gossip about the latest who's-who and what's-what stories of our neighborhood always brightened my day. About a quarter of the way home, I decided I would treat myself to a much needed bubble bath. That morning I had thrown together a pot roast so that the Crock-pot would do the cooking— it was the wedding gift that had become my hands-down favorite. Before all of that though, I would fish out the Mamas and the Papas' record, place it on the stereo, strike a match to the vanilla candle, and sink-chest deep into an ocean of bubbles. The Mamas and Papas and a hot bath were always the perfect panacea for anything.

Upon rounding the last jagged curve, I saw it: his blue Firebird parked in the driveway.

A knot formed in my stomach.

"Gotta run, April. See you tomorrow," I said making a beeline for our house. Mark had made it abundantly clear that he did not like me working, and I didn't intend to give him any ammunition.

"See you, Jules!" she hollered back.

Turning the key in the lock, I opened the door. Inside, Mark sat on the couch, his eyes burning with what was becoming an all-too-familiar look. His rigid body, blood-shot eyes, and tightly clenched hand wrapped so tightly around the glass that it could break at any second sent shivers down my spine. His eyes—those eyes that hypnotized me the first time I'd seen them—were looking more and more like they belonged to a monster.

"Where've you been?"

"At the A&W with April," I calmly replied, praying that this honest response would calm him down.

"Like hell you were." The words left his lips in a peculiarly calm manner, his voice barely above a whisper.

"We stopped by for a black cow after work."

"And why should I believe that?"

"Because it's the truth, Mark...that's why." I started upstairs to our room to hang up my jacket.

There in the middle of the dresser was the letter from my mom, open to the page where she had suggested we find a marriage counselor. In my last letter, I had confided in her about the slap at the Magic Time Machine, and about the change in his personality since his Dad's death and SERE school. My palms became sweaty and my heart began to race. Mark would be furious if he had read it.

The stairs creaked. Slowly. Methodically. Deliberately. Footsteps. One by one. Each step of the ascent getting louder; my head pounded like a war drum, my heart beat wildly and furiously. I hastily refolded the letter, stuffing it in the bottom of my lingerie drawer.

With a loud resounding step at the top, he proclaimed his presence. He leaned against the wall and impaled me with his drunken gaze that settled on my purse now clenched tightly in my hands, pressed against my chest. A useless shield against the stranger standing in front of me.

"I read your mom's letter," he said icily. He paused as if giving me time to digest his words.

Frantically, I tried to think of something that might quiet his fury. "She just wanted to know how everything was going and to let us know they were thinking of coming here to visit us in a couple of weeks when Daddy has his vacation," I sputtered as I grabbed my denim shorts and white tank top from the dresser. I pushed in the drawer with my hip and turned to face Mark. "They've never been to California. I thought it'd be fun to take them to San Juan Capistrano—"

"I know what she said. I read it. Why is she suggesting we see a counselor, Julie? Just what *exactly* have you told her? Our personal lives are just that: personal. You don't go blabbing everything to your mother."

"I don't, Mark. She just happened to call me the other night after that fight at the Officer's Club. My mom just picks up on things. I've told you that before."

"Give me that," he demanded yanking the purse off the dresser, ransacking it before dumping the contents on the floor.

"What're you doing?" I gasped.

"I'm sure you've got some guy's phone number written down in here," he insisted, rummaging frantically through the pieces of paper now strewn across the floor. "I called your parents and informed them that their daughter has been going out to clubs to meet other guys."

"You did *what*?" My voice started to acquire a bitter edge. His random accusation came out of the blue. The nerve of him to tell my parents such hideous lies. My blood began to boil. A fire had been ignited.

"You think I'm an idiot, Julie?" he said, as he yanked me by my hair to spin me around.

I struggled to regain my balance, but he slapped me and I stumbled backward, tripping over the leg of the dresser.

"Mark, stop it!" I pleaded in a strangled voice.

"Shut up. Just shut up!" He grabbed my arms so hard that my fingers started to go numb. "I've heard enough of your lies!"

And as if in slow motion, he started choking me using my waist-long hair as his weapon—wrapping it around my neck, tightening the grip. Frantically, I tried prying his hands away, but I couldn't even scream. He abruptly stopped and stumbled backward. Sweat rolled off his brow and he just stared at me in a cold silence. I scooted away from him, gasping for air, taking short ragged breaths. My throat raw and dry.

That night I lay silently in bed, frozen with fear. Over the past few months of our brief marriage I had experienced a carousel of emotions. Emotions that swiftly jolted me from exhilarating highs to unimaginable, hellish lows. The haunting, twisted, sinister pipe-organ melody could almost be heard playing in the background. Shock. Disbelief. Nothingness. The silent screams were louder than anything I'd ever heard. My chest tightened. How could this be the same man who was always the life of the party wherever he went? The same man who always made me laugh? The charming, intelligent man who would spontaneously burst into a cartwheel in the middle of the room just for kicks? The man who classified everything as a "piece of cake." Who was he, really? The terrifying truth was that I didn't have a clue. I began to question myself. Was it me? Was I in some way provoking him? Was it something I had done, or perhaps failed to do?

Later that night when Mark's breathing went into that slow rhythmic sound that meant he had fallen asleep, I slipped out of bed, painstakingly measuring every movement so as not to make a sound. I held my breath as I closed the door behind me. For several minutes, I stood frozen in front of the bathroom mirror, stunned at my own grim reflection.

To an otherwise rational woman, the choice would have been clear, but the turbulent mixture of overwhelming emotions had become all too familiar. Were they becoming second nature? An acceptance of a destructive cycle consisting of bliss surely followed in time with torment, anguish and heartbreak? Was this to be my future? But how could I even begin to walk away? To leave? To turn my back on the man I loved more than life itself. I gripped tenaciously to the idea that things would get better. But somewhere in the perplexity was the truth that I might be allowing myself to become one of those women who refused to see the reality of what was going on right in front of her.

Reaching down to the second drawer, I methodically, slowly, opened it and quietly rummaged through. My hands brushed across the makeup bag that hadn't seen the light of day in months. It was next to the ornate hand-painted jewelry box my grandmother had given me for my sixteenth birthday. Mark didn't like me to wear makeup. Or jewelry.

The silver handle of the scissors reflected the overhead vanity lights. Grabbing some of my hair with my left hand, I made the first cut right below my chin. I stared at the clump of long hair now hanging limp in my left hand. There was no hesitation after that, and within minutes, the hair that I had grown since high school was gone— eliminating one weapon that Mark had already used against me. Looking at my new reflection, I felt a sense of empowerment at the bold new woman now staring back at me. Not only was my hair gone, but with it, my innocence as well. The idealistic young woman who had entered into a marriage full of hopes and dreams no longer existed. And as badly as I wanted to save my marriage, I refused to be a victim any longer. A new strength was rising up in me that even I had not known was there. There is a fine line between loving someone and losing yourself in the process. Careful not to make a sound, I turned off the bathroom light and quietly slipped beneath the covers.

Once again, lying there in the dark as the moon sliced through the curtains, I found myself making a litany of excuses. I'd always made excuses for him until eventually I had justified his actions. How could I forgive what in an instant had become unforgivable? Don't try to solve it tonight, I consoled myself. Tomorrow will bring clarity. Tomorrow I'll know what to do.

"What did you do to your hair?" he asked with mild disgust as he walked into the kitchen the next morning.

"Do you like it?" I retorted sarcastically, handing him a steaming cup of coffee. Two could play this game. I knew how much he loved my long hair, and I had braced myself for his reaction. Surprisingly though, Mark's response was tempered. He knew good and well my motive for cutting it off.

"Yeah. It looks good on you. I kinda like it," he said, his words forced as he took a bite of toast and pulled out the chair next to me.

I released a breath I hadn't realized I'd been holding.

"Now look who's lying?" I retorted in an attempt to defuse the situation. I poked at my pancakes, my appetite still missing. The hand that had been wrapped around my neck the night before now tenderly rubbed my back in circles. A disguised apology.

We ate the rest of our breakfast in silence. The evening before was never mentioned again but as I stood at the front door watching him pull out of the driveway, I started mulling over the past few months: the bruises I'd thought I'd been hiding so well under the turtleneck and long-sleeve sweaters, the pit in my stomach every time Mark walked through the door, and the conversation with Mr. Bradford last week, when he'd pulled me aside before the lunch crowd trickled in.

"I can see what's been going on," he'd said as he slid into the booth across from me. "No one should put up with abuse, Julie."

I'd averted his gaze...horrified, waves of trepidation
had washed over me. *Abuse.* Hearing the word had somehow made it seem even more real. The shades of denial
finally lifted.

"I know Mr. Bradford. I know you're right. But I love
him," I'd said. I hadn't admitted to anyone that we had
a problem, much less my contemplative thoughts of leaving. I turned to stare out the windows at the lonely parking lot outside. "He's been under a lot of pressure," I had
muttered.

Mr. Bradford gently patted me on the shoulder as he
slid out of the booth. "I'm sure he is, Julie, but you're not
his enemy."

I had stared down at the table, subconsciously twirl-
ing my wedding ring around and around my finger.
Thinking back to that glorious day when Mark had placed
it there. The promise we'd made to each other. It wasn't
that easy, I wanted to tell Mr. Bradford. The black and
white with which he viewed the situation was muddied
with mixed emotions until it was a depressing shade of
grey. If it was all bad, it would have been easy to leave.
What the bruises didn't show was the fluttering of my
heart every time he walked through the door. The way
he looked at me with a passion and desire I had never
known. The crazy, bordering on neurotic inexplicable
pull he had on me.

All I knew right at this moment was that I needed to
get away. I needed some time to think things through.

To somehow find clarity in the midst of chaos. That afternoon, while Mark was at work, April let me borrow her car and I took off down I-15 in her red and white '71 Camaro.

In a daze, I kept driving. Escondido, ¾ mile. Mark and I had been to a park there our first week in California. Drudging through the somewhat familiar overgrown brush with bright green foliage intertwined, I finally found it. The bench that I vaguely remembered appeared in a small clearing a short distance away from the hiking trail. The prolific splattering of orange and pink wildflowers reminded me of the Texas hill country in spring when the Bluebonnets and Indian Paintbrush were in full bloom. Springtime in south Texas is typically a happy time ushering in a sense of hope and promise...a total contrast to the isolation and despair that I was feeling now. Sitting under that gnarled Monterrey Pine I could no longer hold back the tears. Drawing a shaky breath, I slowly started to calm down.

I knew what I had to do. And this time there'd be no turning back. The terror that had pulsed through my veins the night before had high-jacked any hope of trust. The heaviness choked me more severely than Mark's hands had the night before. I couldn't possibly give myself permission once again to forgive him. This time I had to leave.

14

San Diego, California
Fall 1975

April and John had made it clear that I would always be welcome in their home. They were well aware of the bruises. April had asked me about them on more than one occasion, but each time I would avoid answering her and attempt to change the subject.

I knocked on her door. John's large frame loomed in the doorway. He was an intimidating man of 6'3" with a heart of gold. He smiled, sensing a trace of desperation, and held the screen door open. "Hey gal, come on in! April's in the kitchen."

Then he disappeared down the hallway. April was busy putting a casserole in the oven when I walked in.

"Hey girl, you feeling better? It always helps the mood just to hit the road." She said over her shoulder, closing the oven door.

"A little. Thanks for letting me borrow your car. I was wondering if by any chance I might be able to stay with you tonight. Mark and I had another run-in," I said, my face flushed with humiliation.

"Sure, hon," she said in her sweet Georgia accent. April's name suited her, conjuring up visions of soft flowers, sudden storms, and cool evening breezes. "We'll put some dinner on for you. There's plenty to go around. Just grab your things and come right back. I'll have a glass of wine waiting for you."

Mark's car was gone, much to my relief. During the short walk from April's house to mine, I had made a mental checklist of everything I needed to grab, sticking strictly to the bare necessities. I did *not* want to be anywhere close when he returned home. I yanked the overnight bag from the closet and tossed it on the bed, throwing in a couple of t-shirts, tank tops and jeans. Then I headed to the bathroom.

The backdoor creaked. My heart dropped.

"Jules, you home?" Mark called from the bottom of the stairs.

"Yep. I'm home." I strained to sound nonchalant as I continued packing. Like a woman without a care, rather than one who felt as though her whole world was about to implode. He bounded up the steps two at a time.

"Why don't we go out to dinner tonight?" he asked, appearing in the doorway, leaning against the frame, arms crossed in front of his chest. He smelled of Zest soap and English Leather after-shave. His hair, wet. Donning jeans and his Badfinger t-shirt. Why'd he have to look so good?

"I think it's best if we have some time apart, Mark," I said swallowing hard. "I'm staying at April's tonight."

His forehead wrinkled as his gaze shifted to the small brown suitcase on the bed.

"What's going on, Jules? I thought everything was copasetic."

Copasetic, one of his favorite words. A word that couldn't be further from what we were at that moment.

"No, everything is *not* copasetic. You need help, Mark. *We* need help. I can't do this anymore," I said, grabbing the bag and sliding past him.

"What the hell is going on?" he snarled, grabbing me by the arm and spinning me around to face him. It wasn't until he was six inches away from me that I detected the nutty smell of bourbon.

Shaking, the feelings of hurt, anger, and fear bombarded me all at once.

"You can just unpack that damn bag," he commanded. "You're not going anywhere."

I ran downstairs as fast as I could, trying to remember where I'd left my purse and keys. I was surprised to hear him leave out the front door. Fear and panic seized control. The gun in the storage room...was that why he'd gone outside? Survival mode set in. Frantically, I bolted the back door and darted to the front door to lock it as well.

Locked out, he angrily pounded the window adjacent to the front door. I slid down the wall onto the kitchen floor, pulling my legs up tightly to my chest and burying my head in my arms. I prayed that one of our neighbors would hear the jarring sound of breaking glass and call the police.

His bloodied hand reached through the broken pane and turned the lock on the door. Furiously, he marched over to where I was crouched on the floor and grabbed me by my hair, jerking back my neck until my eyes met his.

The grueling naval pilot training meant for war and survival was now being unleashed on me. His enemy was nowhere in sight. Mine, however, was right in front of me. So close that his daggered eyes pierced through me, as sharp as the shards of glass that lay scattered around us.

"Jules, I won't let you leave me." The disdain in his voice only moments ago had contorted into desperation. Fury morphing into despair. He now looked tired and lost. Confused. Sad. The same look that until now had consistently roped me back in...back to the place of forgiveness.

The doorbell rang. A loud voice demanded, "Police! Open up!"

"Stay here," I told Mark. In the ten steps to the front door I managed to swiftly wipe away any evidence of emotion.

"It's police, open up!" the voice boomed even louder.

"Can I help you?" I asked, cracking open the door.

The officer pulled the brim of his cap down, sucked in a breath, and grabbed the pen from his shirt while simultaneously reaching in his back pocket for his pad.

"We had a call about a domestic issue, and from the looks of it, there appears to be quite a disturbance here," the officer said, surveying the glass strewn across the entry and living room floors along with the overturned chair and vase.

The officer's gaze shifted past me to Mark and the bloodied hand that Mark was wrapping with a kitchen towel before settling back on me. "You okay, miss?"

"I'm fine, officer." The words sounded forced.

"Well, it certainly doesn't look that way," he said, pointing to the glass-littered floor. "What exactly happened here?" He chomped noisily on his gum as though it were a substitute for an old tobacco habit and clicked his pen, apparently irritated. "You two married?" "Yes, sir," Mark replied, appearing behind me.

"Can I have your names and a brief description of what happened here tonight?"

"Sure," Mark said, shifting his weight uncomfortably. "It was just a lover's quarrel, officer, but everything's fine now."

"Well, that may be, but I still need to get both your names for my report," he stated emphatically. He turned his gaze toward me and held it there, leaning against the porch railing, his arms crossing his chest. "You sure you're okay, ma'am?"

"I'm fine--," I answered in a beleaguered fashion, trying to feign normalcy before giving him my name.

The officer scrawled my name on his pad before suddenly shifting his gaze to something in the hallway. His brow furrowed. "You fly for the Navy?" he asked Mark, nodding in the direction of his framed F-14 picture hanging on the wall.

"Yes, sir. I do," Mark replied, his charm suddenly back in full force.

And just like that the tables had turned.

"You guys sure are somethin'!" the officer said, shaking his head in amazement. "I always wanted to be a pilot but decided to follow in my old man's footsteps instead." And with that, the officer clicked his pen, stuffed it back in his pocket, and reached forward to shake Mark's hand as though he were some sort of celebrity, never asking for his name.

"Take it easy you two. I enjoyed talkin' to you, but I don't want to have to see you again anytime soon. At least not under these circumstances. Ma'am," he said, tipping his cap before almost skipping down the steps. And just like that, the broken glass, shattered window, and bruises on my neck all became irrelevant. Mark was a Top Gun pilot. All was well with the world. If only it was that easy.

Even though tempers had cooled, tension still charged the air.

"I'm going to go, Mark. I'm exhausted and I think we need to think about things."

I wondered if he was going to object. But he didn't.

"We can talk in the morning," I said, giving him a peck on the cheek.

Grabbing my bags, I walked out into the dark night, gazing up at the many stars. I didn't look back.

15

Fall 1975
San Diego, California

The sight of flashing emergency lights dancing throughout the parking lot, bouncing off the beige stucco cluster of townhomes lured neighbors from the comfort and quiet of their homes. I could feel their stares, and hear their whispers. April and John were waiting for me in front of their house.

"Julie, bless your heart...come on," she said, putting an arm around me in a futile attempt to shield me from the neighbors' prying eyes.

The screen door slammed behind us as we walked into her house. She rushed to turn on a few lights. The warmth did little to assuage the cold, empty feelings.

"Julie, I'm going to put your bag on the chair in the guestroom, okay?" John touched my arm tenderly as though I might break. And I felt as though any second now I might do just that.

"Thanks, John."

"I have a plate ready for you in the oven and a fresh pot of coffee brewing," April's raised voice reverberated from the kitchen.

I mindlessly picked at the chicken and rice casserole, green beans, and crescent roll on my plate. "Thanks, April, everything looks delicious, but I've lost my appetite."

"That's okay, sweetie. You just leave it. Grab that mug, Jules, and pour yourself a cup. Let's go on the back porch. John was just heading off to bed, weren't you hon?"

"As a matter of fact I was. Okay, girl," he said, turning to face me, "you know you can stay here as long as you need to. April's been worried sick about you. You two girls talk and I'll see you in the morning."

Sitting at the opposite end of the couch, thinking about how well she and John got along, and how close she was to the other Navy wives, I hesitated as to whether I should confide in her. As a whole, the Navy community was a close-knit group. Did I dare tell April the extent of what had been happening between Mark and me over the past six months of our marriage? She obviously knew a little, but could I tell her everything? And did I dare tell her my resolve to leave San Diego and Mark? But I desperately needed to talk to someone, and so for the first time, I decided to let my guard down.

April didn't say a word. Instead, her hazel eyes got rounder and rounder with each stunning revelation. I told her about the incident the weekend before our wedding at the Magic Time Machine and how he'd slapped me in front of our entire wedding party for no apparent reason. About the evening at the Officer's Club and how he'd become enraged on the way home, accusing me of liking Pete, when he had initiated the whole dancing thing to begin with. I told her about the talk with Mr. Bradford. And finally, how Mark had reacted to my mom's letter. She reached across the couch and hugged me. There was a sense of relief in having told someone all I'd been going through. Finally, I was able to let go of the secret I'd so carefully been guarding. My body felt drained.

"Julie! I had no idea. You never said a word! Why on earth didn't you tell me before now?"

I blinked hard and bit my lower lip. "I don't know...I haven't told anybody. I'm crazy about him April, but I know I can't stay with him."

"No, you *can't*," she said, shaking her strawberry blond curls and setting her cup of coffee down on the table with a thump.

"This is so much worse than I even imagined," she responded in an equally defiant tone. Raising her chin in an unwavering fashion, she continued. "In fact, you're going to stay right here until you decide exactly how and when you're going to leave that man...and don't you think for one second that I'm taking no for an answer. Tomorrow, John will go with you to get your things and you can stay in our guest room." And as though someone had turned the tenderness switch back on, she grabbed hold of my hands, looked me straight in the eyes, and said in a softer voice, "It's going to be the hardest thing you will ever do in your life. But you're going to *have* to leave him. You are going to *have* to be strong. Mr. Bradford was right. This isn't love, Julie... not real love....you have to realize that."

I stared at her, not really wanting to hear what she was saying. The words cut deeply even though I knew she was right. Her tone was so matter-of-fact, as though all it came down to was a simple little decision. If only. . .

With everything in me, I had desperately wanted to make this marriage work...to make it into the dream that I had envisioned. But I knew that this was no longer an option. My plans to leave Mark had to be set into motion. I could no longer deny the undeniable or excuse the inexcusable.

——— ———

The next morning when I returned home, I poked my head in our bedroom. The sheets were in disarray and the shades drawn. Mark lay sprawled across them, wearing nothing but boxers. He rolled over in bed, hair rumpled and out of place, eyelids struggling to open. There was an empty liter of Coke and an opened bag of peanuts on the nightstand.

"You still asleep?" I asked, inching closer to the bed.

"Jules," Mark groggily replied. "You're home." There was a trace of surprise in his voice. He rolled onto his side, supporting his weight on one arm. He reached across to touch my thigh and stroked it with his thumb.

"Yes."

"For good?" he asked.

"For now." I replied.

Against April and John's advice, I'd made the decision to stay in our home until I left.

"I really am sorry, Jules," he continued with a pained look. His voice sounded oddly different. Almost fragile. Vaguely desperate.

"Haven't you ever had to forgive anyone, Julie?" he asked abruptly, as though he'd been holding on to this thought for a long time. The directness of the question caught me off guard.

"Sure I have," I answered stiffly.

"Then why can't you forgive *me*?"

"I have Mark, over and over again. But everyone has their limits," I responded, resisting the urge to give him the reassurance I knew he was seeking. The moment seemed to linger. Suspended. The sounds around us magnified; the TV he'd left on in the living room, the whirring of the lawn mower next door, and the Johnson children playing basketball down the street.

"I've been thinking, Jules. Why don't we take that drive up to Carmel."

We'd been talking about visiting Carmel ever since we'd arrived in San Diego. Carmel, with its magnificent scenery and mouth-watering cuisine. April and John had recently taken a weekend trip there and told us all about it when they'd returned.

"We need to get away," he said encouragingly, as though a weekend trip would erase all the bad. Erase the times he'd tried to hurt me. To kill me.

"I don't know, Mark," I said flatly.

"Let's go this weekend," he continued, oblivious to my apathetic response.

I smiled back at him, trying to disguise the dread churning from deep within.

By the time Mark left for work, he seemed comfortable that everything was once again fine between us. I put a pot of coffee on, sat down at the table, and buried my head in my hands.

Later that morning, I called my parents but didn't tell them everything. I simply asked Daddy to send me a one-way ticket to come home. He didn't probe any further.

Three excruciating days passed before the ticket finally arrived in the mail. I had asked him to send it to April, ensuring that Mark wouldn't find it. My flight to

San Antonio was scheduled for three o'clock the next afternoon. That morning, the morning of my flight, I pretended to still be asleep while Mark was getting ready for work. When I heard the front door slam, and Mark's keys rattle the stubborn lock, I tiptoed to our bedroom window and parted the red linen drapes I had triumphantly and single-handedly hung six months prior. And as the iridescent hands on the alarm clock slipped to 4:55 a.m., I watched for one last time as Mark, dressed in his fitted brown uniform, marched across the lawn, slipped into his blue Firebird, pulled out of our short driveway, and sped off into the orange and pink rays of the sunrise. I tried to freeze-frame the image, straining to follow his car as far as possible. Moments later he, along with my dreams, vanished into the California sunrise.

The Mayflower moving van was due to be at my home at 8:30. I had explained to the representative my situation and the urgency of being on time and having everything packed in four hours. At 8:35 the doorbell rang. Relief swept through me. By 11:00, everything I owned—everything I'd brought with me to begin my new life with Mark—was packed safely away on the van. Everything, that is, except for his brown leather recliner in the corner, the rabbit-eared T.V., the torn white blouse he'd ripped off the night after returning home from the Officer's Club and his prized F-14 picture that hung in the hall.

How could I set foot on that plane knowing my marriage had failed? My dreams reduced to a smoldering wreckage of a fragmented life that had been broken beyond recognition.

16

San Antonio, Texas
Winter 1975

"American Airlines Flight 451 for San Antonio, now boarding at Gate 7."

"That's you, hon," John said gently, picking up my bag.

I gave April and John a hug and thanked them for all they had done, putting on a brave façade I was certain they could see right through.

"Make sure you call us when you get home, okay?" April said.

"Promise," I replied. My legs were dead weights, anchored down by an invisible force. The world seemed to move in slow motion as I laboriously placed one foot in front of the other. My heart had never felt so heavy, and a wave of nausea hit me as one of the flight attendants greeted me at the door.

I took my seat, lost and in a daze. I no longer felt real. No longer felt alive. Staring out the window, I watched as the ground retreated further and further. My life was disappearing beneath me—the pieces of my world dissolving a little more with each foot that the plane rose. Each mile carrying me further from my dream. Had I made the right decision? My head started to pound until I felt like it was going to explode. Retrieving the bottle of Vanquish out of my purse, I chased a couple down with a glass of water and put on the in-flight headphones, trying to somehow numb the pain. "Oh, Hummingbird" was playing as the tears began to trickle down.

The flight from San Diego to San Antonio forced me to be alone with my thoughts. The watch that Mark had given me for Christmas was still on Pacific Time. Three-thirty. Mark would be arriving home any minute. How would he react knowing that I had left San Diego? That I had left him...

First he would wonder why I didn't greet him at the door. Then, noticing the empty living room, he would have charged up the stairs to our room and found all of my clothes gone. There was no note, no message. I was pretty sure he would call every neighbor he could think of. But first, he'd most likely go over to April and John's. Then he would have called every person that I'd ever talked to or about—frantic to find out where I was, or who I was with. He'd probably even call Cherry and Candy, the strippers who lived two doors down. The whole scenario played out in my mind. This by any definition was hell...my living hell.

I departed the plane to find both of my parents waiting for me.

They didn't ask questions. Mom put her arms around me as Daddy took my bag. I had left San Antonio less than a year ago with everything I owned—the world at my feet. I returned home a mere shell of my former self. How could I not have seen this coming?

The drive home seemed unreal. Thoughts of Mark blurred everything.

That night I tried to sleep. My parents shielded calls throughout the night from Mark, who had by now figured out that I had flown home. I lay awake in my bed for hours. Muffled cries that no one could hear. They came from somewhere deep within. My throat clinched so tightly I felt as though I was suffocating in the darkness. The moon darted in and out amongst the clouds, casting long shadows on the walls. The sheer panels over my bedroom windows seemed eerily still. The hypnotic hum from the wall heater provided the background noise for my thoughts, which endlessly swirled around Mark. Thoughts I wanted to turn off, but couldn't.

St. Gregory's carillon woke me the following morning from my fitful sleep. I rolled over and looked at the clock—8:00 a.m. Three measly hours. The sick feeling in the pit of my stomach from the night before was still there. I stared at the ceiling—the fact that I was back home, stung. Back in my childhood room that was frozen in time with its lilac bedspread and curtains to match. The pink princess phone, a gift from my parents on my 16th birthday was still on my nightstand. The room was much the same as I had left it six years prior when I'd packed my bags for UT. The bulletin board, a smorgasbord of pictures and newspaper clippings from my dance team days and our football's state championship, and the mum Tom had given me to wear at my senior prom, now a petrified gold and brown still hung on the wall beside the Beatles poster. It felt odd lying in this room, as though I was living someone else's reality. Intense emotions were numbing any connection to the outside world. There was nothing to get out of bed for. Every thought began and ended with Mark. Without him, I couldn't breathe.

The phone rang. I scrambled to answer it before my parents did, my legs briefly buckling beneath me. I heard the familiar sound of his breath on the other end and could almost feel its warmth on my neck. Without hearing a word, I knew it was him. My heart beat wildly. My head spun and my hand shook.

"Jules, you there?" he asked in a timid voice from over twelve hundred miles away. And yet the control he had over me, over my emotions, was just as strong as though he were standing right beside me. He pleaded with me, and as hard as I tried to remain mad at him, my defenses crumbled with every word.

My head. My heart. Conflict. Turmoil. Why did he have this much control over me?

"Jules, you know I love you more than anything. You're my entire world. I didn't mean to hurt you, Jules. You've gotta believe me."

"But you did," I said. "Why would you treat someone you supposedly love like that? Why?"

"I don't know, baby...I don't know what got into me. And I'm so sorry. I just got crazy jealous."

"I can't go back, Mark. I'd be a fool—the way you treated me."

"Jules, I'll spend the rest of my life making it up to you...."

His voice trailed off as though he were trying to think of something that would convince me to come back. The sad truth was he didn't really have to say much at all. Just hearing his voice on the other end of the line was proving too much.

"I'll do anything, Jules. I even talked to my mom, and she told me that if I loved anyone as much as I love you, I would do whatever it takes to get you back. Jules, what do I need to do?" he pleaded.

"I don't know Mark. I—"

I put my hand to my forehead and closed my eyes, trying to muster every ounce of courage I had, but I felt my defenses crumbling.

"It can't be the same this time," I finally said.

"It won't be."

"You need counseling, Mark. *We* need counseling."

He was quiet again.

This man, who thrived on the intense adrenaline rush that comes from being catapulted from zero to 160 miles per hour in seconds, launched into total darkness, and coming to a screeching halt on a moving aircraft carrier the size of a football field in the middle of the Pacific ocean, was in reality more terrified of landing on some leather couch in a Zen-like office exploring his feelings with a total stranger.

"I don't need a shrink, Jules. That's your mother talking."

"No, Mark, it's *me* talking. And it's not a shrink, it's a counselor."

"Same difference."

I looked outside. Hetty, with her elaborately decorated straw picture-hat was in her front yard pruning her prized Julia Child rose bushes. Roses that earned her awards every year with the San Antonio Rose Society. George, Hetty's husband, had his hood open and was fiddling with the battery on his Cutlass Supreme. I was sure my dad would be out there any moment to lend a hand. Why did Mark have to make this so damn hard?

"We need help, Mark. And if you're not going to go to counseling with me then I'm not coming back."

There, I'd said it. Drawn a line in the sand. I held my breath, worried he'd call my bluff. He seemed to be getting better at that.

"Fine," he said. "If it means you coming home I'll do it."

"I don't want you saying that just to get me back and then nothing changes," I said emphatically, trying my best to somehow convey to him that there was simply no other option.

"I'm not. I'll go. I promise."

Daddy traipsed across the lawn, jumper cables in hand.

Mark's relentless overtures combined with even more promises to seek counseling at a nearby church, convinced me to go back—to give him, to give us, another try. Maybe I had been too hasty in my decision. I hadn't married him to give up without a fight. And if he was willing to admit he was in the wrong, then I owed it to him—to me— to make sure I had given our marriage a fighting chance.

"Okay," I finally consented.

"Okay?" He repeated, "You'll come back?"

"Yes. But *you're* buying the plane ticket this time."

"Of course."

— ~

"Why on earth, Julie, would you even *think* about going back?" Daddy asked, unable to conceal the severe frustration and intense disdain he now felt for his son-in-law. He shook his head in disgust, forcefully wiping grease off his hands with the gold shammy he'd placed on the plant stand. The Singer sewing machine whirred from the kitchen table where Mom was busy sewing table runners for the church bazaar. She eased her foot off the pedal and placed her glasses on the table.

"You're going back?" she asked, looking up at me, mouth agape. "Julie Elizabeth, what on *earth* are you thinking? The man almost killed you!"

"I don't know, mom."

The answer wasn't good enough I could tell.

"He's under so much pressure mom," I continued. "You and daddy have no idea. It's been a horrible year. And maybe I haven't been understanding enough."

She just scoffed and looked at my dad in a bewildered fashion.

"He doesn't mean to hurt me, mom. I know he doesn't."

"Julie, you're a grown woman and we can't make your decisions for you any longer, but going back to him would be a huge mistake," Daddy said, folding his arms across his chest and leaning back against the countertop.

"It's complicated, Daddy" was my only response that bore even a shred of truth.

"I sure hope you know what you're doing, Julie," my mom interjected while Daddy just turned to wash his hands. The sewing machine once again whirred to life as I left to pack my things.

━ ━

Exactly two days later, I boarded a plane for the flight back to San Diego. Back to Mark. It didn't take long, however, for me to realize that the fear of what he might do was now greater than the damage of what he had already done. A few weeks after returning to San Diego, Mark insisted that we look for a new place to live, to get a fresh start...away from everything...and everyone.

We walked a tight-rope, both of us trying hard not to disturb the calm waters. One afternoon while Mark was at work, April invited me over for lunch. John happened to have off that day. The three of us relaxed outside on their back patio while John fired up the grill for some steaks.

"So, Julie," John said, his back toward me while he was manning the grill, "how are things going between you and Mark? We still can't believe you're back."

"They're okay, I guess." I watched as the condensation slid down the side of my glass of iced tea. "So far, so good."

"Well I'm glad to hear it," he said.

"What have you two been up to on the weekends? We hardly see you around," April asked bluntly, taking a sip of her tea while stretching her long legs in front of her to relish the hot rays of the sun beating down. Even from behind her John Lennon-esque sunglasses, I could see her inquisitive eyes. It was hard to believe that April could have ever been anything but the picture of grace. But, she had once confided in me, her high school years had been spent as an awkward, gawky teenager. You would never guess that now.

"Mark's been itching to move, to get a 'fresh start' as he puts it. I guess he's embarrassed by all the commotion we've caused."

"Well, he should be," she muttered under her breath before taking another long sip. John cast a sideways glance at her.

John, who certainly had already become more involved than he would have liked, came over and set the platter of steaks down in the center of the table and covered them in foil. "Sure he wants to move. He probably would like to move far away. Away from *everyone* you know...but then what, Julie?" John's sharp tone caught me off-guard. "What's he going to do when he's taken you from the only people you know in the entire state?" he continued. "Think about it. It's your decision and your life. We just hate to see you get hurt again."

His biting words hit me hard. Words that echoed my dads. I had a flashback to our last conversation weeks earlier when daddy had stood there in the kitchen, fear and disappointment laced in his words.

The next weekend, we took another house-hunting drive. This time Mark had found an area he wanted to show me that was remote, peaceful, "in the country." However, only twenty minutes into the drive, as we passed a couple of vineyards and old barns, the conversation with John the night before started rumbling loudly in my head. The events of the past six months cascaded into a volcano of emotions.

"Pull over, Mark."

"You okay, Jules?" Mark asked in concern, gently placing a hand on my shoulder.

"I just need some fresh air," I said, leaning my head against the cool glass.

I couldn't live this way. I knew it was only a matter of time before something else would trigger another event.

At the next embankment, he turned off the road and slowed the car to a stop. I got out and tilted my head back to breathe in the fresh air. Focusing on the horses in the nearby pasture as they neighed and galloped in spurts, we both just stood there on the side of the road, leaning back against the car, not saying a word. All the while, I silently wished that we could go back in time. Scoop up all the bad in our hands, letting the Pacific winds carry the ashes of our dreams to the deepest waters of the endless ocean. All that would remain would be the good. The happy times. Because there had been so much good. So much laughter. And so much love.

I glanced over at Mark out of the corner of my eye. The fiery rays of the sunset glinted off his hair. I knew I loved this man more than I had ever loved anyone or would ever love anyone again.

The sun dipped below the horizon, and the moon emerged suspended like a giant milky globe in the evening sky. Six months ago, its' silver luminance would have aroused feelings of giddy romance; now it just seemed to cast a pale, sickly light on the remains of what could have been.

We hadn't reached Mark's destination, but I had reached mine. And although he hadn't laid a hand on me since I had returned home, a gnawing, ever-present fear persisted that he one day would. And so, one month later, I boarded the plane for what I knew would be my second and final trip back home, making a promise to myself that I would never again love anyone with such passion, vulnerability, and trust as I had Mark Jennings.

17

Varenna, Italy
Friday June 13, 2008

When the brochure had cautioned about a "steep incline," it was not exaggerating. With a heave and a groan, Julie climbed the next series of steps that without a doubt would cause even the most seasoned hiker to "feel the burn." As usual, she was beginning to regret her grand ambition.

Zoe would be getting married in fewer than twenty-four hours. The destination wedding had done its job of distracting her. The mystic scenery, the exotic language, the rich food, the hospitable Italian people, and the charm and seduction of a foreign land had all done their job. Gently guiding Julie through yet another transition in her life. Even though Zoe hadn't lived at home since she left for college, her weekend visits had made it seem as though she really wasn't gone. Julie would now officially be an empty nester. Already, the unfamiliar loneliness was creeping in, jolting her back into reality with a cold hard thump. The distractions were no longer there keeping the hope of a restful night's sleep unfulfilled. At last she gave up, washed her face, brushed her teeth, threw her hair up in a loose ponytail, and stuffed her feet into the pair of Aasics now well worn by the gravel over which they'd trodded the past few days. The quarter-mile hike to the Fiumelatte would hopefully help burn off both the calories and the guilt of indulgence in so many carb-filled meals and luxuriant desserts consumed over the past few days.

The others wouldn't be up for another couple of hours. Plenty of time, at least according to the brochure, to complete the hike to the Fiumelatte, a must-see for Julie that the others had foregone in favor of a trip to Villa Balbionella, the famed location of Princess Naboo's retreat in the latest *Stars Wars* movie.

Right now though, with each determined step, her bright idea was feeling less and less brilliant. For inspiration, she imagined Leonardo da Vinci trudging up this same hillside, parting the stray branches that fanned the path and climbing in solitude amongst the birds and butterflies on a quest to answer one of Italy's legendary mysteries: the source of the Fiumelatte. According to his journals, he had been fascinated by the milky river and was determined to uncover its unknown origin. Italy's shortest river appeared each year in early March and disappeared sometime in October. It had been the source of legends and fables and attracted scientific and romantic minds alike.

The low, distant roar of rumbling water gave her the encouragement to continue on. After climbing a few more feet, it came into view. As she took a seat at one of the picnic tables, she found herself grateful that someone had the forethought to provide such a nice place to relax. The low rumble had now been replaced by an ear-splitting whooshing that told of the fury and power of the river as it plummeted down the mountainside. Even after having read numerous descriptions, its frothy white water and imposing strength still came as a surprise. Not at all the trickling stream she'd pictured in her mind.

Flowing over the rocks with fury, the river gained momentum as it continued down its path, reflecting what seemed to be the twists and turns of her life. She leaned her head back, closed her eyes, and listened to the Fiumelatte, soaking in the tranquility of the moment. Marveling in yet another one of God's mysteries. Just as she'd hoped, the hike provided a resurgence of strength and peace.

Two hours later, she joined up with the girls for an afternoon of pampering before the rehearsal dinner. Julie
couldn't help but laugh as she observed that the once
stiletto-clad girls had finally learned the art of survival
in Varenna and were now sporting their athletic shoes.

They briskly wound their way down the tree-lined
promenade to Salon Giarda. The plan was for each of the
girls to enjoy an hour massage followed by pedicures to
match their red tea-length strapless gowns with a flared
skirt. The rich color was chosen to reflect the Italian
culture and had been an instant favorite.

"This is more than a ten-minute walk," Zoe mildly
protested.

"It just seems that way, Zoe, after all the chicken al-
fredo and tiramisu you girls inhaled last night," Julie
joked.

"It was sooooo worth it though," Allie chimed in.

"There it is!" Mindy screeched with delight as the
Salon came into view.

Zoe forced open the heavy wooden door and the
woman sitting at the receptionist desk warmly greeted
everyone.

"Welcome! You must be the Cortisi party. We are
ready for you. Would you like some vino?" the receptionist asked, holding up a bottle of red wine.

"Sure!" the girls answered in unison.

"I love this place already," Zoe said, and everyone
laughed.

The massage tables were all lined up in a row, unlike the dimly lit tranquil rooms she was used to. The fact that the girls were lying face down on a towel did little to inhibit the conversation in any way. The jokes, laughter, and happy recollections flowed throughout the entire hour, and before long, it was time for the pedicures.

"Oh no," Zoe groaned. "I can't believe I forgot my iPod.

"Zoe, why do you need your iPod right now?" Julie asked in exasperation. "We're here to relax!"

"Because, Mom, I thought it'd be fun to listen to some music while we get our pedis done. I know I for one don't understand a word of this Italian music. I mean, it's beautiful and all," she said, flashing a quick, apologetic smile to the owner, "but I want something we can sing along with."

"I brought mine, Zo," Allie said, pleased with herself. She bent down to pick up her purse. See!" She whipped out her iPod triumphantly. "What did you want to listen to?"

"I'll find it," Zoe said, snatching the iPod from her sister's hand and scrolling through the list of tunes. "If You Wanna Be Happy" sounded from the tiny player. Zoe looked at her mom and sister and they burst out laughing while everyone began to belt out the words *"...never make a pretty woman your wife...."*

When the girls were growing up, Friday nights were pizza picnic and movie nights. And hands down, *Mermaids* had been their favorite. Over the years, the girls had worn out the VHS tape. Julie could still see Zoe in her New Kids on the Block pajamas, crimped hair pulled back in a neon-colored scrunchy, and Allie painting her sister's nails in-between bites of popcorn. The girls had a routine of dragging out their sleeping bags to the middle of the living room floor, and a pillow fight at some point always ensued, pounding each other until they'd erupted in a fit of giggles and collapsed in mutual defeat. Zoe and Allie had fought like cats and dogs growing up, but loved each other just as fiercely. She'd always known they'd be close. As close as she and Amy were. And it felt good watching them now, belting out the words horribly off-key. The reminiscent scene made her smile.

The non-stop flurry had begun to take its toll, so when the petite, bubbly assistant made her rounds offering another glass of wine, Julie politely declined.

By four o'clock, everyone was back at the hotel. The rehearsal dinner wasn't until six, and Julie, for one, planned on spending at least a few minutes soaking up some more sun and taking in the view from her balcony.

Pristine white sailboats took to the lake in force. Not a surprise, since the low morning clouds had burned off and the day had turned out to be gorgeous. Birds chirped in the citrus trees and laughter floated up from the veranda below. Maybe it was the lake, or the wedding, but as hard as she tried not to, her thoughts kept drifting back to Mark and the weeks after she'd arrived back home from California...for the final time.

18

San Antonio, Texas
Spring, 1976

or several weeks after returning home, I would wake myself up in the middle of the night crying. Thoughts of Mark held my dreams captive. Although my parents pleaded for me to go to a counselor, I couldn't do it. I wasn't ready to confide in a total stranger. No one would understand. The blinds remained closed in my room at all hours of the day. I wanted no part of the life that continued outside of my four walls. I wanted no part of a life without *him*.

All it would take was one phone call. And I knew that. He would be ecstatic and beg me to come back. It would feel like our honeymoon all over again. But I also knew that the darkness would always be lurking in the background, waiting patiently...it might take a week...a month...or two...but it would always be there. And when I least expected it, the thief would come once again to steal what little of me remained. And so many times, in moments of weakness, my fingers would brush across the phone. Ready to dial the familiar digits of our California phone number. The dichotomy of emotions would come barreling down with the force of a freight train, annihilating everything in its path.

Mark phoned incessantly every day for the first month, but gradually the phone calls became more infrequent, and by the third week of the second month, he had only called twice—on Friday when he had gotten off work—and once, on Sunday night. The friction of conflicting emotions was hard on me. Hearing my dad say each time, "Yes, Mark," frustration souring his normally placid voice. "I'll tell her you called." All the while yearning with desperation to run into the hallway and snatch the phone. Just to hear his voice. I needed him. He had become an addiction. But like any other addiction, it would only be a short-term fix, a momentary high only to set me up for an even greater fall. In some perverse psychological way of thinking, it did bring a small measure of comfort to know that he seemed to be suffering too. But the expanding length of time between calls meant that he was moving on. Adjusting to a life without me. By his own definition—compartmentaliz-ing our life together—effectively filing me away in his past.

If only I could do the same. No matter where I turned, I saw Mark. In the quiet solitude, however, the memories were the loudest. I longed for him, needed him. I closed my eyes and could see that strong jaw line he'd inherited from his father. Feel the coarseness of his hands as his touch melted every part of me.

— ❦ —

A couple of months after returning home, I got an unex-pected call from April.

"Hi, sugar!" she said, her Georgia accent even thicker than I remembered. "You doin' okay? Johnny and I were talkin' 'bout you over dinner last night, and it dawned on me that we hadn't heard from you in quite a while."

"Yeah, I'm doing fine. Just trying to survive the sweltering Texas heat," I laughed, struggling with what to say to her. No sense in spilling my heart out. Besides, I didn't want my drama being the topic of conversation during her early morning jogs or Bingo night at the club with the other Navy wives. April wasn't like that, but I didn't want to take the chance. "How are things there?" I asked, deflecting the question.

"Oh, everything's pretty much the same here. The good news is that the strippers moved out, but the bad news is a couple with a yapping Chihuahua moved in. He's cute, but Jules they leave him out all night. Who knew such a tiny creature could be so dang loud! I'm having to hold John back from marching over there in his boxers and telling them exactly what they can do with their adorable little Snickers."

"Oh no!" I laughed at the image of calm, cool and composed John, losing it over a three pound Chihuahua.

"I never thought I'd say this, but I think I'm actually missing the strippers."

"Oh my God, April. It must really be bad."

"Yes, it's *horrible*."

"I'm sorry, April. Maybe he'll settle down once he gets familiar with his surroundings."

"Lets hope. Well enough of that. We had our annual barbecue last Saturday, but it wasn't the same without you."

I wondered if Mark went. Or more importantly, if he went alone. I didn't dare ask. And April didn't mention it.

"Did you bring your famous potato salad?" I asked. April's potato salad was honestly the best I'd ever had. "I never did get that recipe from you."

"Yes I did, and I'd be more than happy to drop it in the mail!"

"Thanks, I'd love to make it sometime."

Another pause. "Mr. Bradford asked about you the other day. Asked if I'd heard from you."

"Oh?"

"Yep."

Another long, uncomfortable pause.

"I told him I hadn't talked to you in awhile but that the last time we talked you seemed like you were doing better."

"I am. Tell him I said hi."

"I will."

I didn't know what to say. I didn't know what to ask. Part of me wanted to grill her about what Mark had been up to—had she seen him at the Officer's Club—had she seen any women hanging out at his place—*our* place? Did he look as though he was suffering? Or did he look as if he didn't have a care in the world? I wanted to know. And yet I didn't. No matter what she told me, just talking about him would be unbearable.

"So, Jules, how are you really doing?" Her voice became soft, her concern evident over the phone.

I placed a shaky hand on my forehead, rubbed my temples, closed my eyes, and carefully chose my words. "I'm okay I guess. Just taking it one day at a time."

"Are you, Jules? Are you *really* okay?"

I turned to look at the leaves rustling on the branches outside the window. My gaze settled on the turquoise clay pot with yellow sunflowers sporadically painted around the base that I'd made for Mom in fourth grade. She had kept it all these years. An ivy plant now draped over the sides and onto the window sill spanning the width of the ledge. I had never been a very good liar.

"I'm doing better," I said.

April was silent for a moment. I knew she didn't believe me, but being the good friend that she was, she let it
drop, allowing our conversation to end in a lie. I promised to call her in a couple of weeks. Another lie.

I hung up the phone and sat down at the kitchen table, staring out the window. I ached to tell her everything. And to hear every detail about Mark. She and I
had grown so close over the past year. But she lived too
close to Mark. And too far away from me.

19

San Antonio, Texas
Spring 1976

Something inside me had died. I knew that. It had to. It was the only way I could have left. The only way I could find the strength to move forward was to allow a portion of my soul to remain behind—locked in the bittersweet memories of my yesterdays. The hollowness that remained in its place transformed slowly with each passing minute, hour, day, week and month, until the feelings hardened into an invisible force of self-preservation. A shield that nothing and no one would be able to penetrate and destroy ever again. The prospect of dating seemed unfathomable. The divorce had taken what seemed like forever, and for another six months after that I still struggled to get out of bed each morning.

It had been over a year, and yet I still felt vulnerable and knew my ability to trust another man had been sorely damaged. Love was now a lofty ideal reserved for the naïve. Love was disposable—easy come, easy go. Doris Day's mantra, *"Que será, será,"* once said with the vigor of sunshine, innocence, and youth, was now the disillusioned mantra of a woman who had been crushed. A shattered heart is a dangerous thing.

I'd never entertained the idea of dating more than one man at a time. And I certainly wasn't searching for my next great romance. Now, I was going to do what guys did, play the field. No strings attached, and certainly no feelings. I would date so many men that I wouldn't know their past, their history, their families, or even their jobs. And most importantly, I wouldn't care. They would all become intermingled, jumbled into a tangled anonymous web of casual affairs and fleeting flings. There was anonymity in numbers. And safety in anonymity. It wouldn't be about the sex. It wouldn't even be about them. It would be about losing myself in someone else so that hopefully I would forget the pain that lingered deep within. Growing more numb with each reckless encounter. I was determined to hurt men as deeply as they had hurt me. Those were my plans. But even with my most devious intentions, the idea of serial dating was repulsive. It turns out the perpetual good girl mantra was hard to shake.

Eventually, I relented and agreed to see a Christian grief and loss counselor my parents had found. After months spent in therapy with Dr. Thompson, I realized I was going to at some point have to take back control of my life and trust myself again. Gradually, with the dogged encouragement and relentless nagging of friends and co-workers, I reluctantly dipped my toes into the murky waters of the singles scene. Karen, a former co-worker at the hospital, set me up with a close friend of a friend. He was still in med school, and the entire time I learned more than I ever wanted to know about cadavers. Never again would I look at a doctor the same way. And by the time he was finished talking, the perfectly cooked fi-let mignon looked about as appealing as raw oysters. My long list of first dates also included Bob, the shoe sales-man, who seemed to be more taken with my feet than with me. Warren, the engineer, whose preferred topic of conversation always centered on his ex-girlfriend of four years and the heartless way she had broken it off with him just three weeks earlier. There were attorneys, musicians, and construction workers. Most of my dates turned out to be decent guys—great guys. Guys that most girls would have been thanking their lucky stars to have met. But the dates would end almost as quickly as they began. They weren't *him*. At some point, during each and every date, I would find myself wishing I was talking to Mark instead of the man sitting across the table. Wishing that it was Mark I was holding hands with—Mark's eyes I was gazing into.

That is, until I joined the singles co-ed volleyball team at Trinity Baptist Church. That was how I met Danny. Danny Knight was fun, cute, shy, and one heck of a volleyball player. His thick mustache and universal jock appeal was just what the doctor had ordered, the perfect temporary distraction. He had a very giving and kind personality. Showing up at my door with a flower, a necklace he thought would complement my eyes, and an array of spontaneous gifts meant to win my heart. However, Danny would not be a permanent fixture in my life. The truth was he had come along too soon. But what he did teach me was that my calloused heart would be capable of loving again. And perhaps that was the greatest gift Danny could have given me.

On December 9, several nurses decided to go two-stepping after work for some much-needed R&R. The Red Chandelier was a typical Texas dance hall on the edge of town and a hopping place on Friday nights. We arrived so late that the place was only half-full, but the air was still so thick with smoke that it was as though I was looking through foggy windows. An old jukebox on the opposite wall flashed with every color from the rainbow as it played classic country tunes. A few people were singing along to an old Merle Haggard song.

Occupying two-thirds of the stools at the bar, it was obvious that we weren't exactly regulars there. Mary

Ellen, a friend of Karen's and a first-grade teacher at Stephens Elementary, was sporting the quintessential teacher's sweater complete with apples, worms, and a third of the letters from the alphabet splattered along the bottom.

"Would anyone like to join me at a table?" I asked. Anything had to be better than these uncomfortable wooden stools.

"I would!" Lisa said.

"Me too," Mary Ellen chimed in.

The two teachers in the group both raised their hands in agreement. I laughed inwardly. *They really do need to get out more.*

"Boy, am I ever glad you spoke up and suggested this," Lisa said once we were seated. Lisa, a New Jersey transplant, always dressed to the nines for our girls' night out. With her overly teased hair armored by five layers of hairspray and bright red lipstick, she seemed more like an advertisement for a dating show than a nurse. Her long-island accent and flamboyance, which irritated others on the nursing staff, intrigued me. I'd never met anyone quite like her. Her unfiltered, take-it-or-leave-it attitude was refreshing for a change. "The last thing I wanted to do was sit at that dang bar all night," she said.

"Y'all up for some appetizers?" I had heard that the food was supposed to be pretty good.

Lisa's hazel eyes lit up. "That sounds perfect. I'm starving."

We ordered some queso, salsa, and chips, one of the specials, along with two margaritas complete with salt on the rim. I sank back into the booth and eyed the clientele, but so far, the only appealing thing about the dimly lit dance hall was the tall, dark-haired guy leaning against the bar. I had spotted him when we first walked in. His jet black hair and blue eyes reminded me of pictures of my dad when he was in his twenties.

"This just makes me miss Robby even more," Lisa confided, moving aside the teal cocktail umbrella with her perfectly manicured fingernail to take a sip from her Texas-sized margarita. Everyone was well aware of how heartbroken Lisa had been when Robby, her boyfriend of six months, dumped her two weeks earlier for a good friend of hers.

"Well, just don't think about him, if you can help it. This is your night to have fun." It was a lame attempt to console her, but it seemed to help.

"You're right...besides, he's not worth the salt on the rim of my margarita, is he?" she boldy said, raising her half-empty glass in the air.

"No he isn't!" I said, clanking my glass to hers.

"See that guy sitting over there with the brown plaid shirt on?" she asked, abruptly changing the conversation.

I looked over my shoulder in the direction she was pointing.

"The one with the black cowboy hat?"

She nodded, "I've seen him before."

"You have?"

"Yeah, I'm pretty sure he lives in my apartment complex."

"Well then, why don't you ask him to dance? Nothing ventured, nothing gained!" Of course, I would never do the very thing I was so boldly prompting her to do.

"You're right," she said, slamming her hand down on the table as though I had just given the most brilliant advice she'd ever heard. "What's the worst that can happen?" And with that, she flashed an eager grin and stood up.

Confidently, she marched right up to him, margarita in hand, adjusting her skirt along the way. And with a toss of her hair, she did it. He led her onto the dance floor.

"Well, that was certainly fast," Mary Ellen said with a touch of envy, watching as the rugged cowboy in the black hat twirled Lisa around.

I had to admit that I was impressed by Lisa's quick turnaround

"I'd say this calls for another around," Mary Ellen laughed. "You want another margarita?"

"No thanks, I'm good," I responded. "This should last me awhile."

As I watched Lisa sashaying around on the dance floor, a figure in front of me suddenly obscured my view.

The same good-looking guy who had been at the bar only moments earlier was now standing right in front of me. "Is this chair taken? Mind if I join you?" he asked.

"No. I mean, sure! I'd like that."

He was even cuter close up with his black hair and blue eyes. His lightly starched green-collared shirt and pressed black pants indicated that he was not a regular—at least not in your typical run-of-the-mill, blue-collar, rugged-cowboy kind of way. I was startled by my own forward response. The old me would have been coyer, more mysterious.

He settled into the chair and reached across the table to shake my hand. "Hi, I'm Tony. Tony Cortisi. I couldn't help but notice your big blue eyes from the other side of the room."

I found myself blushing. How many other girls had been roped in with that very same line?

"Nice to meet you, Tony. I'm Julie," I responded, shaking his hand.

"So Julie, what brings you to the Red Chandelier?"

"I'm here with some coworkers." I leaned back against the chair. "So what's your excuse, Tony Cortisi? You're not from around here, are you?"

His eyes sparkled when he laughed. "Very perceptive. What gave it away?"

The way he asked indicated that he was unaware that he blended in about as well as Mary Ellen and her alphabet sweater. I didn't know whether to laugh or act shocked. "Oh, just a couple of things...like slacks instead of Wranglers, loafers instead of boots. You know, you're not really sportin' the cowboy look."

"Ahhh...busted. I'm from Rochester. I was trans-ferred here with my job. Some of my buddies dragged me here."

"So what kind of job would transfer you *here*?" I asked. San Antonio wasn't exactly the corporate capital of America.

"I'm a pilot with Trans Worldwide."

A pilot—the words almost stung. I had turned my life over to the Lord and this is who he sends? Another pilot? If this was God's sense of humor, I wasn't laughing. All the progress, all the baby steps, the months of counsel-ing, the hundreds of times I'd reached for the phone but stopped short, the nights I spent on my knees in prayer. Had I really come this far to start over? To fall for the same good looks? Be fed the same lines?

I watched him as he talked. In my experience, it was not the standard mode of operation for pilots to be so reticent in revealing their occupation. To the contrary, they normally boasted about their profession right off the bat. Somehow Tony seemed different though. Mark would've let it slip casually in disguised purposefulness. It was part of his hidden artillery. His charm. His play-book. He oozed cockiness. There had not been a humble or self-conscious bone in his body. But in Tony there was. He didn't meet my gaze in a taunting showdown, but nervously glanced away every few seconds. He wasn't Mark. That much I already knew.

"Oh," was all I could manage. "That's nice." I was eager to change the subject. "So how do you like Texas? Big change, I'm sure."

"Love it...so far anyway. I never realized how much I didn't like cold weather, but then again, I've only been here two weeks."

"Two weeks...wow! Sounds like you might need a tour guide!"

"Have any suggestions?" he laughed, leaning forward.

"As a matter of fact I do. As luck would have it, you are talking to a San Antonio tour guide extraordinaire," I teased.

"Must be my lucky day," he said with a quirky smile, revealing dimples I hadn't noticed until now.

"Okay then, it's settled," I said. "Julie Whitaker at your service, Mr. Cortisi. And just when would you like to start your exciting tour?"

"How does tomorrow sound, Ms. Whitaker? Know of any lunch spots to start off this tour? Just one stipulation...lunch is on me."

"It's a deal," I said with genuine excitement. "No tour of San Antonio would be complete without lunch at Tink-A-Taco."

"Tink-a-what?" he said with a confused look on his face.

"Tink-A-Taco. Twelve o'clock. The first stop on your tour. It's a little hole in the wall restaurant, but when it comes to Mexican food, those are the best kind."

"Well, you're the tour guide extraordinaire," he bantered back, getting a lot of mileage out of my less than humble self-proclaimed title.

"Yes, I am," I said, flashing a confident grin.

I swallowed hard, suddenly aware of where this was heading. *You're just going to have to start taking chances. And allow yourself to make mistakes.* Mr. Thompson's words from our last counseling session came into clear focus. But it was a tough idea to swallow for a woman who didn't trust her intuition at all these days—a woman who was convinced that her own inner "good guy radar" was severely defective. Still, whoever said that this man had to turn out to be Mr. Right? Another lesson learned from Danny. I couldn't go through life comparing everyone to Mark. So, malfunctioning "radar" or not, I would take a chance on Tony Cortisi.

Looking down at my watch, I was startled to see it was already 12:45. My work week had been so hectic and all the non-stop activity was finally catching up to me.

"Tony, it's been fun and I really hate to call it a night, but I'm going to have to run. I'm really looking forward to our lunch date tomorrow, though" I said.

"Already? Wow! You really know how to hurt a guy," he said while pantomiming a stabbing motion at his heart. "Well, can I at least walk you to your car?"

"Sure. I'd like that."

The walk to my car and the peck on my cheek before opening the car door for me confirmed what I already knew. Tony Cortisi wasn't Mark. And as I drove home, I felt a spark igniting that hadn't been lit in a very, very long time.

20

San Antonio, Texas
Spring, 1977

"Y"ou're going to have to help me out here. I can't even pronounce anything on this menu," Tony chuckled the following afternoon. We sat at a secluded booth in the corner of Tink-A-Taco, away from the bustle of the lunch crowd and the blaring Tejano music.

And two minutes later I couldn't stop laughing when he asked the waitress for some more of "that Mexican bread".

"Mexican bread?" asked the waitress, clearly bewildered. She was wearing a hot pink embroidered Mexican dress and a paper flower pin.

"You know," he said, making a circular gesture. "Those round things." He motioned toward another table.

"Tortillas?" I asked, taking a wild guess.

"That's it, tortillas!" he said, exaggerating the double "l" that was supposed to be silent.

"I've never heard anyone call tortillas Mexican bread!" I shook my head, amused by his Yankee cluelessness.

"Tortillas," the waitress repeated with a deep sigh, clearly not amused. She scribbled on her order pad before moving on to another table.

The conversation flowed easily and naturally, as if we had known each other our whole lives, even though we had grown up on opposite sides of the country. Tony and I discussed everything from religion to politics. Fun and easy to talk to, he was the first man since Danny that I didn't want to ditch after a five-minute conversation. His easy-going manner coupled with his striking good looks provoked an excitement that I hadn't felt since Mark. That afternoon, we never ran out of laughter, chips, or tortillas.

Over the next few weeks, Tony and I continued to see each other. Our crazy work schedules somehow paired perfectly. He flew all night with Trans Worldwide and I worked the night shifts, so meeting for breakfast at 7:30

am at Benny's Bagels for coffee and a bagel was the perfect way to wind down after a long night of work. It was during those early morning talks that we began to discover each other.

We went to the movies, Cowboy games (during which I listened politely as he droned on and on about how great the Steelers were), live theatre, the symphony, and had picnics in the park. Without realizing it, I was letting my guard down and allowing myself to fall in love...again.

In March, seven months after we met, Tony asked me to marry him while we were visiting some friends of his in Pensacola, Florida. His off-the-cuff proposal, written in the sand on the shoreline, was just one of many things that endeared me to him even more. It had completely taken me by surprise. But even more surprising had been the adrenaline rush of emotions—the genuine excitement, and unabashed ecstasy—at the thought of a forever with Tony Cortisi.

21

Rochester, New York
Fall 1977

The 1,649 miles to Rochester had gone by fast for me, but Tony had not shared my enthusiasm for taking the scenic route to his home. I had driven the first half, and Tony, the second. Somewhere between Little Rock and Nashville, even I'd begun to question my rationale. But the view once we hit upstate New York made the multiple cups of coffee and one dozen bathroom stops worth it.

"Hey, sleepyhead. You might want to start waking up. We're only about fifteen minutes away from Ma's." Tony's voice nudged me awake. It was interesting that Tony's parents had been married for forty-two years, and his dad was very much alive, but he still referred to his parents' home as "Ma's." I tossed the throw over my shoulder and straightened up.

The highway snaked its way in between gorgeous rolling hills, dairy farms, and wineries. Alternating views of Lake Ontario, meandering rivers, tall evergreens, and cherry trees that burst into flames of red and orange leaves ready to shed their coat for the winter made one not want to blink.

"Wow...it's breathtaking," I said.

I flipped up the visor to check my make-up and ran my fingers through my hair. I had a brief flashback to pulling up in front of Mark's home for the first time, when his dad had startled me. I thought about Mark's mom and his family which of course led to me thinking about Mark. About the genuine excitement and unpolluted dreams I'd once held for the two of us. Taking a deep breath, I exhaled. This wasn't the same. I knew that, but a pit still settled deep within nonetheless. This was it....the much-anticipated moment when I'd come face to face with Tony Cortisi's Italian and very Catholic family.

Fifteen minutes later, we were pulling up in front of a modest red brick and white siding home. Before Tony could even get out of the car, the bright red front door flew open and a petite girl with hair the color of Tony's, sporting the permed style that was all the rage with teenage girls, flew down the steps and lunged into Tony's arms. "Tony! Oh my gosh! Good to see ya!"

"Peanut!" he laughed, returning the hug.

I smiled. Tony had told me all about his younger sister, whose small stature had earned her that moniker. The nickname affectionately bestowed upon the baby of the family by her doting older brothers had stuck throughout the years.

"Peanut, this is Julie," Tony said with a grin.

"Nice to meet you—Maria, right?" I said, giving her a hug.

"Nice to meet chu, too. But it's okay, you can call me Peanut. I've gotten used to it. If you call me Maria, I probably won't even realize you're talking to me. You guys come on in. Ma's in the kitchen baking up your favorite, Tony."

"Cannolis?"

"Is there anything else?" she retorted back. "But no, she's making pierogies. The cannolis are already in the oven."

"Sounds great!"

"And for dessert she whipped up her now famous pepper cookies that she sells to Lombardi's Bakery."

"I know, I heard! She's a bona fide business woman now, huh?"

"Yeah. Dad's not too sure how he feels about that though."

"Fratellino!" a young man's voice boomed from the top of the steps. The similarity couldn't be denied. The same coal black hair, crystal blue eyes, and slightly prominent chin. He had to be Giovanni, Tony's older brother.

"Julie, this is Giovanni," he said, nodding in his direction. "But we all call him Gio!"

Gio held open the door, revealing a receiving line of relatives, the first of whom had to be his dad. He was a tall, thin, white-haired man with a pale complexion. "Tony," he said in a low, raspy voice, engulfing his son in a hug before turning to me. His warm hazel eyes peered down at me as he curled his hands around mine. He had a quiet spirit about him.

"And you must be Julie. It's very nice to meet you, dear!" he said, giving me the same warm embrace that he had his son.

Next, I met Angie, his other sister, along with Auntie Chip and Auntie Lina who had excitedly emerged from the kitchen.

"Oh my God, Tony, let me take a look at chu. Chu've gotten too thin!" Tony's Auntie Chip said, standing on her tip-toes to squeeze Tony's cheeks together before giving him an affectionate sequence of slaps. "What are they feeding you down there, huh? We've got to put some meat on those bones! Come-a-here! Say hello to your Auntie Lina!"

There was no way I was going to remember their names, but I knew I would never forget their faces and the way in which they welcomed me into their hearts.

The aroma of sausage and onions permeated the air, which buzzed with laughter and conversation.

"Franco! What are you doing here, man? Julie, this is my cousin from Pittston, Frankie Barsetti."

"I wasn't about to miss the great homecoming. How long has it been—two, three years? No matter...it's been too long. And this must be Julie," he said, reaching for my hand, giving it a squeeze. "Tony, you sure got yourself a real beauty here," he continued, playfully jabbing Tony on the arm.

"Julie, I hope you know what you're getting yourself into." He pulled away and flashed a huge smile in my direction. "This is one crazy famiglia!"

"Hi, Frankie, it's nice to meet you too," I said. "And yes, I'm quickly finding out what I'm getting myself into," I laughed, shooting Tony a wink over my shoulder. I was already falling under the charm of this flamboyant, lively, raspy-voiced bunch. And just as I was prematurely relishing in the adoration of Tony's family and breathing a sigh of relief that the hard part was over, a short lady with thick gray cropped hair emerged from the kitchen, wiping her hands on a white apron tied around her waist. For a brief moment, I'd forgotten that there was one member of Tony's family that I had yet to meet: his mother. She was far from the frail woman I'd envisioned.

"Antonio!" she proclaimed in a dramatic voice, hands outstretched to cup her son's head in her hands, planting a kiss on both cheeks. "Oh my goodness! Chu've been away too long! I cannot believe chur finally back home!" For a moment, no one else was in the room.

"Ma," Tony said, taking a step back, appearing slightly embarrassed by the lavish affection. "This is Julie," he said, slinging his arm around my shoulders.

"Julie," his mother said, surveying me up and down with a skeptical eye, much like I would imagine she'd pick out her favorite cut of beef at the local market. "Yes. Well, I've certainly heard a lot about you. Welcome to our home." Her lack of enthusiasm was somewhat disconcerting.

"It's very nice to meet you, Mrs. Cortisi."

"Call me, Carmela, dear" she said. "Lei é troppo magra, huh?" she muttered under her breath, casting a questioning glance at Tony.

I looked at Tony, expecting an immediate translation.

"Ma said you're very nice," he fibbed, shrugging his shoulders.

His mother laughed, threw her hands up, and turned back toward the kitchen. "Okay. You two must be starving after chur long drive. So come on in here and let's sit down-uh at the table. You can put chur bags away later."

"Okay, Tony, what'd she really say," I whispered as we all headed into the dining room.

"Ma said she wants to fatten you up," Gio said.

"Ma wants to fatten everyone up!" Peanut added.

"Antonio. Sit down, dear," she said, patting a brown and white chair, motioning to the seat she had pulled out specifically for him. "Antonio, do you want wine or beer?

"Beer's fine, Ma."

"What kind, Antonio?"

"Whatever you have."

She tenderly poured his glass in a frosted mug she retrieved from the freezer.

I took the empty seat next to him.

Cannoli, pierogies, lasagna, and spaghetti graced the long, rectangular table topped with a red and white checkered cloth. There were white pizzas, red pizzas, more food than plates could hold, and more bottles of wine than my Southern Baptist relatives could fathom. The noisy, lively chatter was punctuated with energetic, effervescent hand gestures.

We had been in New York less than twenty-four hours and already I had met more Auntie Chips and Uncle Luccis than I knew what to do with. The ever-animated talking, side-splitting stories, left me inundated and yet happy. Enveloped in a firestorm of hugs and laughter by the boisterous bunch that Tony called family. Thirty different animated conversations took place simultaneously around the dining room table set for twenty-five but at last count had managed to squeeze in thirty. Auntie Chip, now seated to my right, was keeping everybody doubled over with laughter as she recounted her tale of being kicked off the city bus on her recent trip to the local market.

"So there I was. Four bags full of salamis, pepperonis and grapefruit. I go to put the change in, and whatd'ya know—"

"The salami falls on the floor!" Auntie Lina chimed in, finishing her sister's sentence.

"No! Ma!" Tony's cousin covered her eyes and shook her head. "What chu do then?"

"What chu think I did? I bent down to pick it up—"

"And the grapefruit falls out of the bag rolling down the steps of the bus," Auntie Lina chimed in again.

Is this an Italian thing? I had to wonder.

Auntie Chip continued, "Not only does it roll out—"

"It rolls down the steps and into the street," Lina finished again, gesturing wildly.

"So I run after it while Chip bends down to pick up the change, slapping the bus driver on the back of the head with the other stick of salami that's protruding from her bag."

"Oh, Ma, you didn't!" Teresa said, raising her hands in exasperation. "Tell me you didn't." The sisters' voices were now raised at least a decibel higher as they strained to be heard above the roar of laughter from everyone at the table.

"She did, Reesa! As God is my witness. I wanted to crawl under that darn bus," Lina said. "But that's not the worst of it."

"You mean, there's more?" Teresa quizzed, horrified.

"The bus driver, after getting slapped upside the head for the third time with that salami, he finally yells, 'Lady....off my bus!'"

"The nerve!" Teresa says, switching on a dime from humiliation to irritation that someone would have the audacity to throw her mother off the bus. The rest of the family, however, was doubled over in laughter, wiping their eyes with their rose-colored napkins.

It didn't take me long to realize that Auntie Chip and Auntie Lina were more like twins than sisters. They had gone from sharing a room as children, to marrying brothers, living next door to each other, producing babies at the same time, and even finished each other's thoughts and sentences. And it was also how I discovered that Uncle Tito, who was actually just a close family friend, had spent two months in jail for embezzlement. Unjustly, at least according to the Barsetti clan. And during the next two hours, I would hear more nun stories from Tony and Giovanni than the Pope heard confessions.

For some reason, Dean Martin's "Mambo Italiano" played in my head and I half-expected a line of shiny coal black Lincolns to pull up in front. Peter Clemenza would strut up the driveway flanked by Marlon Brando and Al Pacino. They wouldn't knock. No. That was not their style. Peter would march on over to Uncle Tito, place a condescending hand on his shoulder, and with a swift nod in the direction of Al and Marlon, proclaim, "Leave the gun. Take the cannoli." *The Godfather* no longer seemed so farfetched. Nope. If they had studied Tony's family when preparing for the movie, they couldn't have nailed it any better. Except for on the big screen, I had never seen anything like them. And usually everything's exaggerated in Hollywood. Not this time. Tony hadn't prepared me either during the thirty-six hours it had taken us to drive here.

Halfway through dessert, Carmela turned to me and asked, "Julie, dear. Antonio tells me you're divorced?" Her chin was lifted and her head slightly cocked, a single eyebrow raised. I focused on the steep angle of the arch, amazed that so much could be conveyed with no words at all.

Suddenly, ten different ninety-mile-an-hour conversations came to a grinding halt as everyone's attention swung towards me.

"Yes, I was married once before," I said softly.

Tony cleared his throat. "Ma, we already discussed this."

"It's okay, Tony," I said, the bite of white pizza getting stuck in my throat as I forced a smile.

"So you're not Catholic?" A wave of disapproval splashed over her face, as mine became bright red.

One would have thought I had admitted to committing murder. Or that I had just disclosed that I had three legs. Carmela raised both eyebrows, this time at Tony's dad. He just shrugged and kept on eating. She sighed exaggeratedly at his lack of support.

"I'm Christian."

"But not Catholic?" his mom reiterated.

The room became even quieter. Everyone squirmed uncomfortably in their seats, their gazes darting about the table. For the first time since my arrival, I noticed that the fridge made a slight clanking noise and that someone had left the T.V. on in the den. Ed McMahon's voice boomed his signature, "Heeeeeere's *Johnny!*" I hadn't realized it was so late.

"Ma!" Tony raised his voice. "I told cha she's Christian."

"But not Catholic," she said once again, saying the words more slowly this time, enunciating each syllable, as though if I wasn't Catholic, I may as well have been a Satanist.

"No, ma'am, I'm actually Methodist."

"Ma! That's enough!" Tony said sternly. "Well, since everyone's here, this looks like the perfect time to tell you guys that I've asked Julie to marry me."

Several of his clan gasped. I could almost hear Carmela stifling her inward silent screams.

Apparently Tony was on some mission, determined to pour more fuel on the fire. I sank lower in my chair.

"And she said yes," Tony said defiantly, pulling me close and planting a kiss on my cheek.

It seemed like an eternity before Auntie Chip broke the silence. "Oh, Antonio, this is wonderful news! This calls for a toast! Giovanni, make sure everyone has enough wine! "

"And fill them to the top, Gio!" Auntie Lina said. "This calls for a celebration!"

"I've suddenly lost my appetite," Carmela said between clenched teeth, slamming her napkin onto the table with a force that made the wine glasses clank before storming out of the room.

My face burned even brighter, hot with humiliation and anger. I might as well have had a scarlet "A" emblazed on my chest. I felt a connection and empathy for Hester Prynne that had been lacking in high school.

"Don't worry, Jules," he whispered. "She'll come around."

I wasn't so sure.

Auntie Chip raised her wine glass first and everyone else followed. "Here's to Tony and Julie. May your marriage be blessed with many beautiful bambinos." I swallowed hard and decided to refrain from divulging the truth about my divorce and endometriosis diagnosis, fearing that if Carmela Cortisi caught even the slightest hint that not only had I been married once before, but we would not be contributing to the continuation of the Cortisi blood line, I might just find myself, along with my bags, tossed out onto the fresh fallen snow. I prayed that Tony wouldn't say anything either. And he didn't.

Here-heres came from the by now slightly inebriated group, and I was never so thankful half an hour later to turn in for the night. A pinch of sadness gripped my heart as I brushed my teeth and changed out of my clothes. My mind drifted back to the table, back to the whole evening. Aside from the obvious fact that I was the last woman on earth his mother would ever have hoped to hold the title of Mrs. Antonio Luigi Cortisi, I too had my reservations. After all, I didn't like the way his mother coddled him as though he was completely incapable of doing anything himself. One step inside the Cortisi home and he inexplicably lost total use of his arms and legs. She had even pulled out his chair for him. Laid his napkin in his lap. His glass was never more than half-empty when she would rush to fill it up. And when Tony had muttered halfway through dinner that he needed more Parmesan, I had never seen someone fly so fast across the room to retrieve a bowl of cheese from the fridge.

I had the sudden urge to escape the room, escape the house. The questions raced through my mind faster than the speed with which the wine had been poured only an hour before. Would it always be like this? Would she ever accept the fact that I was divorced and wasn't Catholic? Was this just the beginning of another endless journey of questions without answers? Problems, real or perceived, that could never be solved?

That night, as I slid underneath the mounds of pink cotton sheets, I stole a quick glance over at Peanut snoring faintly. Must be nice! The Virgin Mother gazed down at me from the top shelf of her dresser. I pulled the sheets up tighter around my neck. Even the Holy Mother herself seemed to be in complete agreement with Carmela Cortisi; peering down at me as she held my numerous sins and indiscretions against me—in spite of the angelic smile painted on her porcelain face. There was no escaping it.

22

San Antonio, Texas
July 14, 1978

O n a warm July evening, the church bells at the Little Church of La Villita seemed to ring with the promise and hope of a new beginning. Much to the dismay of Carmela Cortisi, at half past six in the evening, Tony and I exchanged our vows in front of close family and friends. Half of the names on our invites looked as though they belonged in the cast of *The Godfather*. Reluctantly, the matriarch of the family had resigned herself to the fact that her beloved son was determined to enter into what she considered to be an unholy union— with or without his mother's blessing.

Two months after returning home from our honeymoon, I began having unexplainable bouts of nausea. My whole body seemed to be falling apart. I was weak and tired. A couple of weeks passed with no change in my physical or emotional state before my mother had insisted that I pay a visit to her physician. After listening to my symptoms, along with my self-diagnosed hypothesis, he twisted his gold-cross pen and started scribbling a prescription on his pad to treat food poisoning.

He handed me the piece of paper, leaned back against the cabinet, folded his arms in front of him, and asked a question that hit me right in the gut. "Julie, I know this is a stretch, but is it possible that you could be pregnant?"

I focused on his gold-framed credentials that hung on the far side of the room. What happened to his prediction that I had a one-in-a-million chance of ever getting pregnant? I thought about reminding him about the scheduled hysterectomy in a few months, but didn't.

"That's impossible," I said instead.

"I know that's what I told you, but I'd still like to rule it out before discussing other treatment options. I'd hate to prescribe something in the remote chance that you are. When was the date of your last period?"

"I don't know," I replied, practically choking on the words, still reeling from the shock of his question. I became dizzy just thinking about the possibility. "It's been a while."

Dr. Mason put the clipboard down on the counter, removed his glasses and dropped them in his coat pocket.

"Ellen will set you up for the test, and she'll call you with the results in the next couple of days." He walked out the door, then poked his head back in. "And hold off on having that script filled until we get your results back."

"I will. Thank you, doctor."

As I walked out of the office, I thought about the difficult conversation I'd had with Tony a month into our relationship. I had wanted him to understand that I would never be able to have a child of my own, that we would never be able to have a child together. I had worried so much about how he would take the news, but it hadn't seemed to faze him in the slightest. "We can always adopt" was all he'd said with a shrug.

I felt butterflies of anticipation at the mere suggestion that I could be pregnant. The impossible, perhaps not so impossible after all. I decided not to tell Tony until I knew for sure. Instead of going straight home, I dropped by my parents.

Amy sat in the living room, glued to *The Young and the Restless*. She didn't even notice that I had walked in. I sat down next to her on the couch and watched the last five minutes of the episode.

"Hey, Jules. What are you doing here?" Amy asked during the commercial break, surprised to see me.

"I was in the area. Where's Mom?"

"She's having coffee at Betty's to see Ann's new baby. Why, what's going on? You look a little funny." Amy had inherited our mother's keen sense of intuition that was usually, annoyingly, right on target. The enviable gift had unfortunately skipped over me.

"I went to Dr. Mason today."

"And? Everything okay?"

"They're running some tests...They think I might be pregnant." I couldn't believe I had said it. Just like that. It felt like I was giving it credence.

"Oh my goodness, JuJu! That's awesome!" she shrieked, bounding off the couch and enveloping me in a bear hug.

The front door creaked open. "Jules, you're here! I've got a bag of figs for you," Mom said, heading in the direction of the kitchen. "Betty gave me strict instructions to give them only to you since she knows how much you like them. Did you already have that appointment with Dr. Mason today?" She emerged from the kitchen and looked at us, puzzled at the huge grins on her daughters' faces. "What's up with you two?"

"Yes, he gave me something for nausea," I paused in dramatic fashion, letting the moment build. "But he told me to hold off on filling it for a couple of days. He thinks I might be pregnant, Mom!"

Her eyes grew bigger than Amy's. A tiny sparkle of euphoria briefly fluttered in her eyes. But, it disappeared just as quickly. And as though someone had held up a 'proceed with caution' sign, my mother's expression came crashing back down to earth. "Well, that can't be!" she stated emphatically, worried that he was getting her older daughter's hopes up. "Did you remind

Dr. Mason about the hysterectomy he has scheduled for you in June?"

"Anything's possible, Mom," I said, a little disappointed by her tentative response. I knew she was just trying to protect me, but I'd hoped she'd be a little more excited.

"Well, let's not count our chickens before they hatch. We need to wait for the results to come in," she said. But before walking out of the kitchen, she squeezed me tight and then plopped the brown paper bag filled with ripe figs in my hands.

— ◦ —

Two days later, Dr. Mason called me himself.

"Julie, I know this is going to come as a huge shock, but you are indeed pregnant. So don't fill that prescription. In the meantime, just keep saltine crackers and weak tea on hand."

Suddenly, exhilaration coursed through my body. Feelings of sunshine seemed to radiate outward as if through an invisible prism, illuminating the small kitchen and its bright yellow walls.

That evening when Tony arrived home from work, I told him everything. After recovering from the initial shock, it didn't take him any time at all to call his entire family with the good news.

— ◦ —

And so, exactly one day after our first anniversary as husband and wife, on July 15, 1979, Alexandria Noel Cortisi entered the world at 7:27 p.m. Thirty-six and a half hours of grueling labor, but the end result was a beautiful baby girl we nicknamed Allie. With a peaches-and-cream complexion and clear blue eyes, she already seemed wise beyond her years.

When Allie was just three months old, Tony and I both went back to work. Tony accepted a position as co-pilot on the 737 with Frontier Airlines and I returned to my nursing position at the Methodist Hospital.

Neither of us anticipated the strain that our opposing work schedules and his long absences would place on our young family. Life as a wife and new mother proved harder than I imagined, but also more rewarding. I looked forward to our eleven o'clock feedings. The soft flickering light from the television screen filled up the living room as a new man slowly romanced his way into my life. In the evenings, I would turn on *The Rockford Files* starring James Garner. I knew he was a stand-in, but James didn't seem to mind filling in on those lonely nights when Tony was away.

At two o'clock in the morning, however, there were no such salacious distractions. The ticking of the antique clock that had belonged to my grandparents seemed much louder in those early morning hours. The silence was deafening and the solitude crowded my thoughts. Was I simply suffering from postpartum depression or had I made another colossal mistake in marrying Tony?

Eighteen years loomed in front of me. Endless, cold, and deep.... like the thoughts that gripped me...and the fears that were starting to hold me captive.

Fortunately, Allie was a sweet-natured baby who demanded only the normal amount of routine care and nurturing. I'd heard horror stories of other children who, by their very nature, drove everyone around them to total despair. Colicky babies through no fault of their own seemed to never be satisfied or content. However, the fact remained that the relentless demands of working full time and raising a baby were enough to test the fortitude and character of even the most saintly of women— a status to which I would never come close to aspiring. Motherhood had come as a complete and total surprise, and all I could do was hope and pray that my best efforts would prove to be enough.

Between my job at the Methodist Hospital, taking care of an infant, and Tony's long commutes, depression started to take hold. Although Tony never voiced anything, I sensed a silent separation happening and didn't know what to make of it. With our conflicting work schedules, time seemed to be passing us both by. Days turned into weeks, and weeks turned into months. The malls were now transitioning for the Christmas holiday, decked out in red and green décor. Tony Bennet and Frank Sinatra filled the cinnamon scented stores with their holiday hits. It was my favorite time of year, and yet for the first time in a long time I could've cared less. It wasn't Tony's fault, and it wasn't mine, it was just the way things were. The old cliché, 'two strangers passing in the night' was turning out to be not so cliché after all.

One solitary afternoon while doing laundry, I discovered a note in Tony's pocket hastily scribbled in flowery handwriting on a beverage napkin, 'Hey Tony, thanks for lunch. Call me when you're back in San Fran. Thinking of you, Marcy.' Suddenly, I was seized by a sickness in my stomach that no amount of saltine crackers or weak tea could alleviate. My mind escalated the note to explicit scenarios that played out in my imagination, whose lewd, lurid speculations knew no boundaries.

I marched up the stairs and furiously yanked a few of his shirts from their hangers and stuffed some of his belongings in his flight bag, a stray sock protruding sadly from the side, dragged it downstairs, and placed it outside the door with a note on top saying "Call Marcy" taped to the beverage napkin.

Then I turned the deadbolt.

That evening, Tony banged on the front door for half an hour, demanding that I let him in. He of course denied any knowledge of the note, exclaiming from the other side of the door, "You think if I knew about that note I would have left it in my pocket for you to find? You really think I'm that stupid, Julie? For heaven's sake, just let me in! You're being ridiculous." I just stood there with my back against the door, half of me wanting to open it and the other half of me still furious.   He eventually gave up and left. Where he went, I have no clue. And furthermore I didn't care.

Amy came over that night after I put Allie to bed. I'd called her, hoping a little sisterly advice and fresh insight might help me gain some clarity. I poured us a glass of wine.

"Okay, Jules. Spill the beans. What gives?" she said, sitting Indian style on the couch.

"It's Tony."

"What about Tony?"

"I think he's having an affair."

Amy practically spit out her wine. "Tony, an affair? Why do you think that?"

I told her about the note I found in his flight bag.

"A note? That's it?"

"There've been calls to the house where I answer and they hang up. He seems more withdrawn. Like he's lost interest."

She was quiet.

"Just a lot of things. You know what they say about flight attendants and pilots, Amy."

"Well, have you *asked* him?" she asked, taking another sip.

"Of course I have! He denies everything. Said he didn't even know about any note. But come on Amy, what else would you expect him to say."

"Well, I still think you're over-reacting, Jules."

"Over-reacting?" I didn't know whether to be incensed by her assessment or relieved that she honestly didn't think there was any validity to it.

"I just feel like I made another *huge* mistake. I tried so hard to do the right thing and yet I feel like I'm right

back at square one. And now I've got Allie. I'm just
overwhelmed—with everything. I can't see my way out," I
said, burying my face in my hands.

"Any way out? Jules, Tony's *not* Mark. Everyone can
see that. Tony loves you. I'm sure it's hard with an infant, and with him being gone all the time, but things
will get better," she said handing me a Kleenex she pulled
from her purse.

"What if he's having an affair, Amy? What if he's
making a fool out of me?"

"He's not. It's *Tony*, for crying out loud!" Her voice
uncharacteristically rose to a higher decibel. It was obvious she truly believed that Tony wasn't capable of what I
was so blatantly accusing him of.

"He's a man, Amy! Don't be so damn naïve."

She flinched at my brusque tone. "I'm not *naïve*,
Julie. I just don't think that every man is a cheat and
a liar. There are good guys out there and I truly think
Tony is one of those."

I didn't say anything. I couldn't expect her to
understand—she hadn't gone through anything! How
could she even have a clue what this felt like? She and
Dave had been together since their junior year in high
school. She'd lived such a sheltered, seemingly perfect
life while mine seemed to implode at every turn. Even
now, when I was at the pinnacle of happiness.

After she left that night, I thought about what she
said. And maybe she was right. Maybe I was making
a mountain out of a mole-hill. I tried to reason with

myself and turned on the TV flipping through the channels before settling on *Mork and Mindy*. Robin Williams always made me laugh. I turned off the lamp, letting the glow from the TV illuminate the room, laid down on the couch, remote in hand, and shortly thereafter fell asleep.

～ ～

An out of the blue and totally unexpected call from Mark the following week, only served to punctuate the tumultuous feelings I'd been experiencing over the past few months. It had been five years since I'd last heard from him and I was surprised by how quickly old wounds were ripped open. Wounds I thought had healed so well that the scars were now invisible to the naked eye. Those first couple of years after leaving San Diego there hadn't been a day that passed by without thoughts of Mark. And yet, after marrying Tony, he'd almost become a rare afterthought. A memory only conjured up when Roberta Flack's soulful voice carried across the radio waves or when I subconsciously detected a faint hint of Mark's favorite aftershave, English Leather, as a stranger breezed by in the mall. But now I realized that the wounds hadn't completely healed after all. The countless shaky first steps in my new life—as a wife, a mother—now seemed futile. Just as an earthquake can level in seconds a grand old city that was centuries in the making, just the sound of Mark's voice was enough to erase the last three years.

Suddenly, I was right back on that plane, watching my world disappear as I ascended into the sky.

The initial ecstasy of hearing his voice was rapidly replaced by raw, bleeding emotions. He had wanted to see me, talk to me, and hold me. He asked me to go to California one more time before he left for his tour of duty. He told me he had never stopped loving me. It took all the strength I had left to tell him no...to tell him goodbye. I hung up feeling drained, lifeless. Where had I found the strength? Everything in me wanted to catch the next flight to California. To have his arms wrapped around me one more time.

The cosmic gears of the universe clicked into place, forcing these two events to transpire at one vulnerable moment, catapulting me back to a dark place. A place I thought I had left behind years ago. When had I become a stranger in my own world? Instantly I found myself thrust backward in time. The confidence I had worked so hard to rebuild was crumbling.

I was barely hanging on by a thread, and hour by hour it became more difficult to understand why Allie wouldn't be better off without me. The voices grew louder and I listened more intently. The thoughts became more intense, deeper—until I was drowning, suffocating in them. Tony, the one who helped me learn to love again, trust again, had betrayed me as well. Only one solution for my life remained, and that was to end it. To end the pain. So on a cold winter night in January, I made another decision. And I was convinced it was the right one. The only one.

The bottle of Quaalude sitting on my nightstand was full. Dr. Mason had written the prescription during my last visit, after I had explained my difficulty falling asleep. The prescription had been filled just last Friday. If one could put me to sleep, then I had to believe that taking a whole bottle would silence the pain forever. Quietly, methodically, my thoughts turned briefly to my mom, dad, Amy, and Allie. But they had each other... they'd be fine...everyone would be fine.

With tears streaming down my face, I picked up the open bottle. I turned the light off before reaching for the glass of water. Suddenly, a light appeared in the corner of my bedroom—the size of a dime. The light became larger until it lit up the room so brilliantly that it was almost blinding. My mind raced and my heart pounded, yet I was transfixed. What was happening? A figure appeared in the center of the light. This happened to other people, not to me. But the thoughts stopped. As if in a trance I just listened, although no words were being spoken. But still I listened. And watched. Spellbound.

The figure looked like me and was wearing my favorite red shirt and signature faded jeans. It became clear that this luminous figure standing less than three feet away indeed looked exactly like me. In her left arm, she was holding a baby who looked like Allie with dark black hair, and clinging tightly to her right leg was a curly-haired blonde little girl around the age of four, perhaps five. The figure was radiant, with happy, piercing blue eyes that looked past me into my heart...into my very soul. Her message was clear. Unmistakable. God had a purpose for my life and He had much more planned for me. This wasn't the end. And in time I would understand everything.

Instantly, just as suddenly as she had appeared, the luminous figure was gone, leaving me in shock...in awe. After consulting with a local pastor and reading Charles Capps', "The Ministry of Angels", I realized that the figure who appeared to me that night was actually an angel sent by God—disguised to look like myself, so as not to frighten me. That momentary vision had transformed more than the room. It had indelibly altered my life. God had loved me enough to reach down from heaven and touch me in all my brokenness—at a time in my life when I felt undeserving of His forgiveness, much less his love. But He did love me in spite of my sins. It wasn't until that moment that I knew that His grace and mercy covered my divorce and my hurt. I had been angry at God. Angrier still at myself. But now I realized that if God could forgive me and love me this much, then certainly I could choose to love and forgive myself, as well as Tony.

The phenomenon I had just experienced was one of those larger-than-life moments of transcendence. But its cryptic meaning would remain a mystery until the fall of 1982, almost four years later, when I gave birth to my second child, Zoe Elizabeth. A beautiful girl who was the spitting image of Tony. It was then that I fully realized what the angel had shown me on that dark night. The black haired baby in her arms had been Zoe and the young girl with blond curls standing by her side was actually Allie. God had more planned for me and He wasn't finished with me yet. The prophetic vision with the angel filled me with hope and would forever change the course of my life.

23

Fall 1982
San Antonio, Texas

And as second children almost always are, Zoe Elizabeth, would prove to be the exact opposite of her older sister. The funny, vivacious toddler soon had us packing our bags for Denver, where Tony could be home in the evenings to help. I was realizing my limits, and a move to Colorado was just what the doctor, and my therapist, ordered.

In Colorado, we were happy. Very happy. We joined an Assemblies of God church after an invitation by one of Tony's coworkers who taught Sunday school there. Tony's commute was now a thing of the past and we all enjoyed having him home more often. Although I missed my parents, they made it a point to drive up for a visit every couple of months.

On the advice of Dr. Thompson, my counselor, we decided to make our move more like an adventure, exploring different little towns in the mountains on the weekends. Over the next year, we managed to visit almost every small town outside of Denver, with Georgetown, Steamboat Springs, and Vail topping our list of favorites. Our new life agreed with all of us. From the first snowfall to the piling on of winter gear every morning before school, the whole experience was full of new firsts.

— —

It was during one of those October weekend ski trips to Winter Park that I would discover something that would send all of our lives spiraling in an unexpected direction. After a long day at the slopes, I'd been looking forward to a nice warm shower to soothe my aching muscles. The girls of course went first, and then it was my turn.

"Julie, you almost ready?" Tony poked his head in the door a few minutes later, knowing good and well that if the shower was still running, I was nowhere near ready to go.

With a sigh, I decided to pick up my pace. After washing my face, then my neck, my left arm and my breast, something unfamiliar caught my attention. I froze. A

K . C .   H A R D Y

huge lump! I slid my hand over it again, only slower this time. I turned off the water and reached for the towel.

"Tony, can you come here for a second!" I hollered, cracking the shower door open slightly.

"What do you need, Julie?"

"Just please come here for a second," I repeated.

Within a few seconds, his head popped in. Noticing the look of concern, he came all the way in and shut the door. "What's wrong?" he asked, his brow furrowed.

"Do you feel something here?" I took his hand and placed it where I had felt the lump in the shower.

He was quiet before responding, "Yes, but it's probably nothing."

"You're right," I said, wanting to believe him. It was probably nothing. Maybe I'd bruised myself rearranging Allie's bedroom last week.

"But it wouldn't hurt to have someone take a look," he added.

"I'll do that when we get back," I said, readjusting the towel and unzipping the make-up case. I decided to put it out of my mind.

The rest of the evening we enjoyed what little time we had left of our weekend excursion with no more thought given to the lump. In fact, I didn't give it much thought at all over the next several months. It was easy to do with the hustle and bustle of birthdays and the holiday season approaching. Besides, I had just visited my gynecologist right before moving to Denver. I'd had a leaky discharge from my left breast since Allie was born. But he'd reassured me that there was "absolutely nothing to worry about." He couldn't be wrong...could he?

We celebrated many milestones in our new home. Then, after the holidays, a throbbing pain started to emanate from the lump that still had not gone away.

It might have been a mistake to confide in my mother about the lump. I knew better. Ever since October, she'd been nagging me during our weekly phone calls and the conversations always played out the same:

"Jules, sweetheart. Have you had that lump checked out?"

"No. Not yet, Mom."

"Well, you need to."

"I know."

"If you're not going to think of yourself, then you need to think of your girls."

"It's nothing, Mom."

"Well, you still need to get that *nothing* checked out."

"I will. I promise."

I finally gave in and agreed to see someone on our next visit home in February. Our plans were to drop off the kids with my parents and continue on to Cancun for Valentine's Day.

Even though the flight to San Antonio was booked to capacity, we managed to get the last four seats. However, the following afternoon Tony and I were not as lucky. The flights to Cancun were oversold. And when the ticket agent started recruiting volunteers to give up their seats in return for a voucher, my fears were confirmed.

We would not be going to Cancun. This was one of the disappointing drawbacks of flying stand-by.

The upside of not getting on the flight was that I could now keep my promise to my mother and have the lump checked out by Dr. Mason.

— ～

Which was exactly what I did the next day. Thankfully, Dr. Mason had a cancellation and was able to fit me in on short notice.

The nurse led me down the narrow hallway to an exam room. I sat down on one of the two hard plastic chairs, avoiding the examining chair that loomed on the opposite side of the room. Tony took the seat next to me.

The nurse sat down on the doctor's stool and thumbed through my chart. She looked up, "Denver?" she asked in a sharp tone as she reviewed my paperwork. "Why on earth are you coming to us if you now live in Denver?"

Her terseness caught me off guard. I missed Holly, Dr. Mason's nurse who had retired a couple of years ago. I found myself defending the reason for my office visit to a complete stranger. "We just moved to Denver and Dr. Mason has been our family doctor forever," I responded shortly.

"A mammogram?" she continued in the same condescending tone. "We don't authorize those until you're at least forty!"

"Well then, just forget it. I don't need to see him."
Agitated, I got up to leave, fed up with her attitude.

"Sit back down," Tony demanded, in a tone usually
reserved for our youngest daughter, before turning to the
nurse. "Look, we have an appointment to see Dr. Mason,
and we're not going anywhere until we do just that!"

The confrontation must have aroused the attention
of the doctor because within seconds, he was standing
right in front of us. "Julie," he greeted me warmly. "It's
so good to see you again! And this must be Tony."

"Nice to meet you, Dr.," Tony said, shaking Dr.
Mason's hand.

"Likewise. Now I understand you have a lump you're
concerned about?" he asked with his hands on his hips.

"Yes, sir. It's on my breast."

"Well let me step out for a second so you can change
into this," he said, handing me a pale blue gown. "I'll
take a look at it."

A few minutes later he came back in, put his clipboard on the counter adjacent to the small sink, sat down
on the black vinyl stool, and wheeled across the floor until he was directly in front of me.

"Okay, so where is this lump?"

I placed my hand on my left breast.

He examined the area. "How long have you been
aware of this?" His forehead wrinkled in concern.

"For a few months now. I really haven't been all that
worried about it but figured since I was in town I'd have
it checked out," I said nervously.

"I'm pretty sure that you have nothing to worry about, but I'm going to go ahead and send you upstairs to a friend of mine to be on the safe side—he's one of the top general surgeons in town. His name is Michael Smith. He'll take good care of you. He'll probably request a mammogram right off the bat. Then we'll go from there. I'm sure everything's going to be fine; but it's better to be safe than sorry."

And with that, he wheeled around on the stool, picked up the clipboard, and jotted down the doctor's number on a prescription pad.

"Thank you, Doctor," Tony said taking the piece of paper from Dr. Mason.

"We're actually supposed to leave in the morning for Denver. Do you think we should just reschedule?" I interjected.

"This isn't something you want to put off, Julie," Dr. Mason said, before exiting the room, closing the door behind him.

"What do you think?" I asked Tony as we waited for the elevator.

Tony's eyes remained fixed on the lighted numbers indicating the elevator was descending from the twelfth floor. Both his hands stuffed in his pockets.

"We'll just have to see what he says," he shrugged in an unconvincing fashion. "But I'm sure it's nothing to worry about."

The room was a stark contrast to Dr. Mason's office. The blaringly white walls and white plastic chairs gave off a cold and sterile feel. The single plant, wilting away on the corner of the side table, was the only sign of life.

"Mrs. Cortisi?" a young girl with cropped dirty-blonde hair, who couldn't have been more than twenty years old, asked as she slid back the glass partition. "Dr. Smith's expecting you."

She led me to exam room three. Moments later a tall, very thin man donning green surgical scrubs strolled in. "Well, Mrs. Cortisi, Dr. Mason caught me right before I was about to leave. I understand you're living in Denver now and are supposed to go back in the morning?"

"Yes sir, that's the plan."

"Well, let's see if we can get you out of here then. This shouldn't take too long."

His easygoing manner and relaxed tone was a relief.

"Now show me exactly where this lump is." He was silent as his hands moved over the area. "And how long have you noticed this?" he asked, briefly looking up at me above his black-rimmed readers.

"About six months."

"Is it painful?"

"Yes. But it's more of a throbbing, sporadic pain."

"Well, that's actually a pretty good sign. In fact, with that symptom I'm eighty-five percent sure it's not breast cancer."

Breast cancer? For whatever reason, cancer had never once entered my mind. I had assumed that it was just another sebaceous cyst that had to be removed. I'd had several since early childhood.

"I always like to err on the side of caution though, so I'm still going to send you down for a mammogram. Once you're done, I want you to come back up here and we'll go over the results together."

After several X-rays and exams, Dr. Smith ordered a biopsy. That evening, Tony cancelled our flight.

At 7:30 a.m. the next morning, the biopsy was performed. And by 8:15, the doctor walked into the recovery room and uttered four words that would forever change my life.

24

San Antonio, Texas
February, 1985

*L*ying on the stretcher, I slowly opened my eyes—faintly remembering where I was and why I was there.

"Mrs. Cortisi...can you hear me...can you start waking up for me? How are you feeling?" The nurse in the recovery room seemed to be in a far off distant place.

My mind was foggy. The bright lights overhead were blinding. I could faintly make out the outline of the person talking to me as she continued, "Dr. Smith will be here in a few minutes. Would you like some ice chips?"

"Yes, please," I said. Everything was coming back... the lump...the biopsy. Why I was here...

Dr. Smith's tall outline emerged from behind the curtain. His easy-going nature from the evening before had been replaced by a very business-like tone. It gave me an unsettling feeling.

"Mrs. Cortisi, how are you feeling?" he said as he inhaled a deep breath, exhaling slowly. "There's no easy way to say this...so I'm just going to be frank with you. The biopsy was malignant."

Malignant? I stared at him in disbelief. Maybe I heard him wrong. Maybe all this medication was playing tricks on my mind.

He shoved his hands in the pockets of his white doctor's coat, and shrugged in a bewildered fashion. "I'm sorry. I was certain it was benign. I want you to meet me in my office tomorrow morning so we can discuss treatment options," he said, patting my hand in a consoling manner.

His words hit me fast and hard. They seemed hollow and far away, drowned out by my own mind's monologue. *Cancer*...how could that be? I had just turned thirty-six. I had two young daughters—three and six. God couldn't take me away from them. He just couldn't. I was their mother. They needed me. I had to be there for them. This couldn't be happening...I felt overwhelmed, powerless.

"I'm going to talk to your husband and family now. They'll be in to see you shortly. And I'll see you in the morning," he said, with one final pat on my shoulder.

Cancer? The words swirled around in my head and traveled down to my stomach. A wave of nausea gripped me and I started throwing up.

The nurse shoved a pink plastic bowl into my hands.

"The doctor ordered something for nausea just in case," she said, empathetically. You hang on to this, and I'll go grab the shot from the cart."

I was sweating profusely and my head was pounding. I overheard Dr. Smith talking outside the room, telling Tony that he wanted to see us back in his office the following morning. They talked in a hushed tone, and with the anesthesia still heavy in my system, I lay back on the bed and closed my eyes, praying that when I awoke, I would discover that it was all just a dream...one incredibly realistic terrifying nightmare. I would tell Tony the story over coffee at breakfast and both of us would wonder what it meant, and I would finally say after a few minutes of solemn contemplation, "I'm so thankful it was only a dream."

The beeping of the I.V. machine, and a loud irritating voice over the intercom system, stirred me from my fitful rest. My eyes felt heavy as I opened them to see Tony sitting in the chair next to my bed, lost in his own thoughts. *Not a dream.*

I stared at him, begging for answers I knew he didn't have.

"You're going to beat this, Julie. Your parents and I are going to pull out all the stops."

I could only hope that he was right and wished I felt a sliver of the same confidence.

Three hours later, I was cleared to go home. The attendant brought the wheelchair, and for the first time I saw my parents and Amy. Their eyes were red and swollen but they managed a forced smile. As they reached down and hugged me, I started to cry for the first time since receiving the devastating diagnosis.

"Don't worry, Jules," my mom said. "Everything's going to be okay."

"Oh my God, Mom, I can't believe this! What am I going to do?"

"You're going to beat this, that's what you're going to do," she said with the same matter of fact tone that she had used on my first day at the new middle school. I had convinced myself on that hot September morning that I would spend my lunch hour completely by myself. "You're going to flash that beautiful smile and make friends, Julie," she'd said with an air of certainty. She'd been right back then and I drew some comfort from her unwavering confidence she was displaying now.

Panic and shock were closing in. I was lost in a storm in uncharted waters that I had no idea how to navigate.

Tony was quiet on the drive home. Uncharacteristically transparent, his face etched with trepidation and fear. He caught me looking at him and winked, placing his hand on my shoulder, giving it a squeeze. "I'm going to call Frontier when I get home. I'm sure they'll give me some time off after I explain what's going on."

Still reeling from the news, I couldn't touch the peppered steak, garlic mashed potatoes, and green beans my parents had picked up from Luby's cafeteria on the way home.

"What time are you meeting with the doctor in the morning, JuJu?" Amy's words brought me back to the dinner table. She hadn't called me by my childhood nickname in years.

Allie, who was old enough to understand that something was going on, stared intently at me from across the table, looking for reassurance that everything was going to be okay. While three-year old Zoe, who was sitting contentedly next to her aunt, chewed away on her dinner roll.

"Nine o'clock," Tony answered. "Dr. Smith arranged for us to meet with Dr. Morris, a plastic surgeon who is supposed to be the best."

"A plastic surgeon? Why do I need to see a plastic surgeon?" I asked, taking a sip of the sweet iced tea.

"Let's not borrow trouble," my dad said. "You're in good hands, so let's just hear what the doctors have to say."

After dinner, Amy and I settled onto the back porch swing, while mom tucked the girls into bed. "JuJu, I just know you're going to be okay. God's not going to let anything happen to you," she said, giving me a hug. "Besides, us Whitaker girls are tougher than nails." She pretended to flex her muscles.

I just laughed, thinking back over all those years.
Even though she had filled out as she'd gotten older, she
still had a model-thin frame that seemed immune to all
the cheeseburgers and double chocolate malts she threw
its way. Almost five years younger we'd fought like cats
and dogs growing up, but at the time those five years
might as well have been fifty. I felt bad about that now.
As the teenage years enveloped both of us in our love
for all things Beatles, the gulf between us had collapsed,
and we'd been best friends ever since. I missed our daily
talks. It felt good to have her here now.

The nostalgic sweet smell from a neighbor's fireplace
reminded me of Christmas. The back screen door swung
several times before finally coming to a halt as Mom
came out to join us. The iridescent backyard light cast
long willowy shadows across the lawn. Mom wedged herself between Amy and I on the wooden swing that hung
from the hundred-year-old oak. The three of us sat there
swaying slightly back and forth, looking up at the clear
night sky. The swing creaked tiredly. Zipping up my
jacket against the sting of the cold February air, I tried in
vain to collect my thoughts.

Listening to the melody of the nighttime songs,
I looked around the backyard. A memory haunted every corner. The hula hoop contests Amy and I had held
on the concrete patio. The red juice and black seeds of
the watermelon my dad would split open on the picnic
table every summer when my aunt, uncle, and cousins

came down from Tennessee. The crisp, clean, cool feel of Daddy's shirts that I would help my mom attach with clothespins to the wire clothesline every Saturday before darting off to play with my friends. And in the spring, I would spend hours picking up pecans from the tree my dad and I had planted when I was five. And Mr. Buttons, our black cocker spaniel who was my very first lesson on life, love, and loss, was buried in the patch of grass between the pecan tree and the shed.

"Julie, I'm going to find every book there is about cancer. And I'm going to ask everyone I know to pray for you." My mother reached for my hands and clasped them tightly in both of hers. Her voice took on a pleading tone. "You know that God loves you and wants the best for you. He wants you to be healed. Jesus will never leave your side. You know that is true, Julie."

"Mom's right," Amy said. "You're going to beat this—I just know you will, Jules."

My faith had grown so much stronger over the past couple of years. The visit with the angel had drawn me closer to God. In fact, I couldn't help but wonder if the reason for the visit with the angel was meant to encourage me during this time. I knew that the Lord could heal me, but nonetheless sometimes my fears would take center stage. Doubts would creep in.

"Why's this happening to me...why me? The girls are so young, Mom. I just have to be here to watch them grow up. I can't..." I collapsed in her lap.

She held me tightly, stroking my hair. Amy put her arms around both of us. We sat that way for a long time. In total silence.

"Thanks for everything," I mumbled softly. "I couldn't make it through this without both of you."

"That's what we're here for, Jules."

"We're going to beat this together," Mom said, while rubbing my back in a circular motion, the way she had when I was a little girl and had trouble falling asleep.

"I love y'all." Even as the words left my lips, they seemed so inadequate.

"We love you more, sweetheart."

The following morning, the waiting room felt even colder than before.

"Mrs. Cortisi? Dr. Smith's ready for you now." The nurse took us back to the same room we'd visited the day before. But today everything looked and seemed different.

Addressing both of us, Dr. Smith wasted no time and started right in. "I'm going to get right to the point. You've got a three-centimeter carcinoma. You don't want that hanging around longer than it already has. From the size of it, it's been growing for up to ten years. Julie, as I see it, you only have one option, and that is to have a modified radical mastectomy. I would also highly recommend that you have immediate reconstruction because of your age. Here's the card of an oncologist I recommend. He'll most likely suggest six to eighteen months of chemotherapy following the surgery."

His words were strange and foreign. Medical jargon I knew nothing about. It was a lot to digest, like being in a foreign country without a translator or a map. I wanted to leave the country but couldn't. I was terrified—lonely—isolated.

"Nevertheless," he continued, "Dr. Morris, the plastic surgeon, has agreed to see you as soon as we're finished here. In my opinion, he's the best in his field. He'll discuss further options with you and explain in greater detail the reconstruction process."

My panic must have been more transparent than I thought, and his voice took on a softer tone. "I know you're frightened, but there's always hope—you've got a wonderful support system and that means a lot with the kind of battle you're facing. I know you want more answers, but I can't really tell you more until I get in there and see what's going on."

Tony's eyes mirrored my own. "What do *you* think?" he asked the doctor. "What are the chances that it has spread?"

"There's no way of knowing for sure. I don't even want to venture a guess at this point."

"How long will I be in the hospital?" I asked.

"Three to four days if all goes well. And I feel quite confident that it will. One thing that you have on your side is your age. And you're in great shape otherwise.

However, if you choose to have the immediate recon-struction, then the surgery and recovery both will take a little longer, but it's smarter in the long run than to wait and have to go back in again later."

He sat there for a moment, letting us soak everything in.

"Well, if you don't have any more questions, I'll go ahead and let you meet with Dr. Morris. After you talk with him and decide which way you want to go in terms of reconstruction, let me know so we can schedule your surgery as soon as possible."

Clutching the directions to Dr. Morris's office, we walked toward the elevator in silence and waited for it to reach our floor. The doors opened and a mother with two children close to Zoe and Allie's age emerged. They laughed, carefree, as they entered the pediatrician's of-fice that was across the hall from Dr. Smiths. A slight twinge of jealousy entered my thoughts.

Less than forty-eight hours earlier, that had been me.

25

San Antonio, Texas
1985

D r. Morris was the complete opposite of Dr. Smith. His dark, brooding looks and emerald eyes seemed more suited for a starring role in *General Hospital*. After hearing Dr. Smith's stellar recommendation, I had expected a man with years of experience behind him and a few token gray hairs that backed it up. But it soon became obvious to me why he had referred him.

We talked about the different options surrounding my mastectomy. We talked about immediate reconstruction. And we talked about the long and difficult road to recovery. Physical therapy, I was told, would be necessary to regain full range of motion in the affected arm. I watched films and videos about all the things that should go right, and all the things that could go wrong. My mind was reeling from the massive amount of information being hurled at me. Although they said that it was my decision, I felt as though the decision had already been made for me. I was going to have a mastectomy and immediate reconstruction. There was really no time to think about everything, and maybe that was a good thing.

What we didn't talk about were all the what-ifs. What if I wouldn't be there for all the firsts in my girls' lives? What if I wouldn't be there for their first piano or dance recitals, to meet their first boyfriends, to help mend their broken hearts, to watch them walk across the stage to receive their diplomas, or to see their dad walk them down the aisle at their weddings? What if I missed everything? What if...?

Those questions everyone secretly asks themselves but somehow carefully manage to avoid ever asking out loud. There was still so much left to do...so much life left to experience. The girls were still forming who they one day would become. And I wanted to be a part of that. I *had* to be a part of everything. After all, I was their mother. I was their cheerleader when they were taking their first steps. I was the one who had wiped away their tears and kissed their wounds. It was me who tucked them in every night, read them their bedtime stories, and taught them how to pray. And it was me at 3:30 in the morning, chasing away the monsters that they were certain were lurking under their bed. Zoe might not even remember me at all one day—after all, she was only three. I was not ready to be reduced to vague memories, to mere pictures in a photo album.

The mastectomy itself was scheduled for two weeks later. That would give us time to return to Denver to tie up loose ends. Frontier had generously given Tony one month off. My parents were more than willing to watch the girls as Tony and I headed back to Colorado. In the short time we had lived there, we both had fallen in love with Denver. The decision to move back to San Antonio was not an easy one, but we knew it was the right one. The doctor had made it crystal clear that I would need the support of family and friends during this process, especially since Tony was a pilot and our children were so young.

The next few weeks became a whirlwind of activity. In Denver, we once again packed everything we owned and arranged for it to be shipped back to San Antonio. We notified the school where Allie attended that we would be moving. We made the decision to temporarily move in with my parents. Their home was a small two-bedroom, one-bath, which for an indefinite amount of time would now house four adults, two children, and a cat named Misty. Tony and I would stay in my childhood room, while the girls would sleep in the den on an air mattress. Our furniture and belongings would have to go into several storage units. We enrolled Allie in the elementary school within walking distance of my parents' home. And as luck would have it, Zoe made a new little friend across the street, Lori, whose mom operated a daycare center out of her home. I signed Zoe up. Even though our lives had been turned upside down, we were all determined to find a way to help the girls retain some sense of normalcy.

While Tony and I were busy with the logistics of the move to San Antonio, my mother was doing just as she had promised—gathering every book and article she could find on how to survive breast cancer, and calling every church she could think of to ask for prayers and support. With her stern conviction, she was determined to help me beat cancer. She was my biggest ally. She was also a strong believer in miracles and the power of prayer.

During those two weeks, however, one book in particular caught my mother's attention—Dodie Osteen's *Healed of Cancer*. She was the wife of the renowned pastor of Lakewood Church, and the book chronicled her battle with and victory over pancreatic cancer. It contained a wealth of healing scriptures. Those healing scriptures were the first thing I read in the morning and the last thing I read before going to sleep at night. Once again I started journaling for the first time since I had scribbled in my top-secret diary in fifth grade. Only this time, my musings weren't about the lightheartedness of my youth, playing spin the bottle behind the cypress tree, or the thrill of my secret crush on the boy next door. This time, the words I wrote held the key to my future. They were the secret to life itself and I knew in my heart that God's word would not return void. I believed that Jesus would heal me.

I wrote down scripture after scripture of God's promises. "Verily I say unto you, Whatsoever ye shall bind on earth shall be bound in heaven; and whatsoever ye shall loose on earth shall be loosed in heaven" (Matthew 18:18 KJV). This meant that I could take authority over the sickness in my body. "But he was wounded for our transgressions, he was bruised for our iniquities: the chastisement of our peace was upon him; and with his stripes we are healed" (Isaiah 53:5 KJV). I knew that Jesus had taken my disease and there was no need for me to bear it any longer. I laid the cancer at his feet. By his stripes I *was* healed. The word of God was multiplying in my heart and my faith was growing by leaps and bounds. Like a child with a security blanket, my journal filled with healing scriptures became my constant companion. Everywhere I went, it was clutched tightly in my hand or tucked away in my purse.

And the morning of my mastectomy, as I walked into the Methodist Hospital, I gripped tightly to both my Bible and my journal as never before.

"What's that you're reading?" nurses and orderlies would ask, pointing to the small red book.

"Healing scriptures," I would reply.

"Oh, that's nice" was the typical response with a hint of skepticism.

I understood. It wasn't long ago that I had been in their shoes. It seemed like just yesterday when I was at the University of Texas at Austin, questioning everything I'd been taught to believe in. I became leery of those students on campus carrying their Bibles around, preaching Salvation, while the theory of evolution and Darwinism was being crammed down my throat. Philosophy professors lectured on how theology and world religions were established by men. It was as though overnight I started doubting every aspect of Christianity. From the virgin birth of Jesus to His resurrection. It had been easy to shelve my faith. I was young, impressionable and painfully naïve. But now, as the nurse wheeled me down the hall, I felt a sense of peace, a peace that no one understood, not even me. A peace that certainly surpassed all understanding. I was so thankful that He is a God of second chances.

"Jules!" my mother called from the hallway, running to my side as fast as she could.

She reached out and grabbed my hand. My mother, who was always early for everything, was late. She must have a very good reason.

But nothing could have surprised me more than when she said, "I am so sorry I'm late, sweetheart, but Dodie Osteen called me just as I was going out the door."

Dodie Osteen? How on earth did she get a hold of my mother?

Noticing my surprise, she said, "Dodie said that Tony had asked David Andrews, his co-pilot, to pray for you.

Well, David's pastor is John Osteen, Dodie's husband. The entire congregation at Lakewood prayed for you last night during their evening service. Julie, she told me that there was a word of knowledge that you will live and declare the works of the Lord....that every test will surprise the doctors and radiologist!" She couldn't get the words out fast enough. Her eyes were dancing with enthusiasm and hope. It was a look I hadn't seen in my mother's eyes since the diagnosis.

"Thanks Mom. Don't worry...I'm going to be fine," I said.

"We have to go now, Mrs. Cortisi," the nurse said.

My mom kissed my forehead, and with that I was wheeled through the green double doors of the operating room.

"Well, young lady, you must be Julie Cortisi. I'm Dr. Nelson—your anesthesiologist. You ready for your cocktail?" he asked with a wink.

"As ready as I'll ever be, I guess."

"I'm going to be here the whole time, Julie," he reassured me, gently patting my arm. "Now when the anesthesia sets in you'll start to feel sleepy. Before you know it, you'll be waking up in recovery and this whole thing will be behind you."

I glanced up at the bright lights overhead one last time and thought about how stark and clean everything looked—with everyone donning their caps and blue masks that covered their faces. *This is it.* My eyelids were suddenly heavy.

Managing a faint smile for Dr. Nelson, I noticed the gold ring that bore a cross on the third finger of his right hand. It was the last thing I remembered.

— ~

"Julie, can you try and wake up for me? I'm going to take your temperature." The recovery nurse's voice was loud and jarring.

I strained to open my eyes. The sounds around me were jumbled. Questions swirled around in my head. But I was too sedated to ask them.

"Dr. Smith should be in to see you in a few minutes," she said.

I closed my eyes and drifted back to sleep.

"Julie," Dr. Smith's voice roused me. "Everything looked really good. You came through with flying colors. We were able to get the entire tumor. And the really great news is that the cancer had not spread to the lymph nodes. We took thirty-four nodes and they were all clear....pretty amazing considering the size of your tumor."

Relief washed over me. "That's wonderful. Thank you, thank you for everything."

"Hey, how's our girl doing?" Dr. Nelson, the anesthesiologist, poked his head in the room. "Excuse me for interrupting, but I just wanted to let you know, Julie, that it certainly looks as though all of the prayers for you have been answered and you and I both know who's responsible for that," he said with a wink, his index finger pointing up. "Hopefully, I won't be seeing you anytime soon." He took my hand and gave it a squeeze. "You take care of yourself and have a speedy recovery."

"Thank you, Dr. Nelson."

"We're taking you to the third floor now," the orderly said as he unlocked the brakes on the stretcher.

Dr. Nelson's words were still reverberating in my mind and my spirits were soaring. Tony, my parents, and Amy were all waiting outside in the hallway and walked alongside my stretcher to the elevator.

"We heard the wonderful news, Julie," my mom said, beaming.

"Jules...it's all over with," Tony said, bending down to kiss me on the cheek.

— ⁓

The next morning, there were two taps before the door swung open. "Good morning! How's my favorite patient doing?" Dr. Morris, clad in his green surgical scrubs, asked as he approached the side of my bed, moving the tray aside. "You look like you're doing great, Julie...the question is, how are you feeling?"

I shrugged. "Okay, I guess."

"I need you to raise your arm for me."

I raised my right arm.

"No. I mean this arm," he said, patting my left hand. He folded his arms across his chest and waited.

I tried. I tried again. To my horror, I couldn't raise my left arm. No matter how hard I tried, it didn't budge. It felt as though it wasn't even attached to my body. A look of panic flashed on my face.

"Don't worry—that's normal. We did major damage after removing all those lymph nodes and other tissue. As you know, your body's in shock. We'll start you on some exercises and will have a physical therapist visit you twice a day while you're in here. You'll have to continue the exercises once you get home." He lifted part of the dressing and the bandage, looked it over, checked the drain, and then asked the nurse to reapply the tape.

"They'll get you up tomorrow. Then, Friday, we'll take pictures of your entire body—bone scans, brain scans, you name it, we're scanning it. In the meantime, you get some rest." He turned to shake Tony's hand. "Take care of our girl."

The fact that I knew post-surgery routines well didn't make it any easier or less painful. And it was different being on this side of the bed. Amy, a teacher, always groaned about how teacher's kids were the worst to teach. The same held true in my profession. Taking care of fellow nurses was always an interesting challenge.

As Dr. Morris had predicted, the next four days were filled with physical therapy, X-rays, tests, and walking. Excruciating therapeutic exercises, such as "climbing the walls" with my fingers, and squeezing a small blue rubber ball filled my days. Even the simplest tasks were exhausting. But success was measured in small increments.

Slowly I was improving and by Friday afternoon I was ready to be dismissed.

The reality of what happened didn't sink in though, immediately. *That* didn't happen until I changed the dressings for the first time, unveiling a truth I hadn't fully allowed myself to reflect upon until now. There was only one way to get through this and that was facing it head on—I had to take it one hour—one day—at a time. I refused to think too far into the future. Refused to dwell on the fact that I just had one of my breasts removed. That was minor in comparison to what I was facing. Staying alive was my new priority. And if that meant that I would lose a breast, it didn't mean that I would lose my identity as a woman, or my self-worth. I was extremely thankful that I had been encouraged to have the immediate reconstruction. Although it was not pleasant to deal with the tissue expander, and it took months of painful weekly visits to stretch my skin to the right size, the end results were well worth it. Now it was time to focus all of my thoughts on healing and getting stronger.

Days turned into weeks, weeks into months, and life slowly began to return to normal for the Cortisi family— a new normal, because we all knew that nothing would ever really be the same. Several months and countless hours of physical therapy would pass before I felt like myself again—and even longer before even one hour passed without the stark reminder of what I was going through. I was facing the biggest battle of my life. And occasionally, out of the blue, when I would least expect it, fear would come sweeping in. But it was during those times—during my darkest hours—that I clung to God's word—His promises.

After my mastectomy, church took on an even deeper significance than before. I wanted to thank God for restoring my health, my life, my future. For giving me time. Precious time. One Sunday morning in particular the choir started singing an old familiar hymn—a hymn that was one of my dad's favorites. As Tony and I stood there in the pew singing along, the words moved deep within and uncontrollably the tears started to fall:

> *When peace, like a river, attendeth my way, and sorrows like sea billows roll; Whatever my lot, thou has taught me to say...it is well, it is well with my soul...*

26

Varenna, Italy
June 15, 2008

"Julie!" Jenny called from the other side of the hotel room door early the next morning.

Julie tied the belt around her robe, readjusted the towel on her head, and scurried to open the door.

"It's Jenny."

"I know who it is, silly goose!" Julie said, fumbling with the bolt.

Jenny stood there holding a bottle of Chianti and two wine glasses.

"Well you certainly came along at the right time!

"That's what cousins are for!"

Julie was thankful that Jenny and Ken had been able to make it. Amy was so disappointed that Todd, Amy's oldest son, had his high school graduation scheduled for the very same weekend.

"I was just reminiscing about our days in Colorado when Zoe was a little girl—I honestly don't know where all the years have gone," Julie said, sitting down on the edge of the bed.

"Yeah, the time has flown hasn't it?" Tears formed in Jenny's eyes, and her tone was melancholic. This surprised Julie. After all, Jenny was not the sentimental type. The take-charge mentality always guided everything she did. If there was one word that perfectly suited Jenny, it was strong. During her first divorce, and the death of her mother, emotions had always remained in check.

She abruptly turned around and placed the wine bottle down on the dresser with a thump, keeping her back to Julie. "Do you remember those days of playing 'I spy' in the woods behind Mimi and Poppy's?" Jenny asked as she poured the wine into the two glasses.

"Do I remember? Are you kidding? How could I ever forget that, Agent Snoops! Those summers were some of my favorite childhood memories!"

"Same here!" she laughed.

"Why don't we go out on the balcony?" Julie asked.

"Roger that, Agent Rock Candy," she said, handing Julie a glass. With that Julie followed Jenny out onto the balcony.

"We only have one more day to soak up this gorgeous view!" Julie remarked.

"Makes you a little dissatisfied with the Gulf Coast, huh?" Jenny said.

"A *little*?" Julie scoffed, leaning her head back to take another sip.

For the next hour, they talked just like they used to while swinging on Mimi and Poppy's front porch at 611 Park Street, Paris, Tennessee. That white wicker swing had heard it all. Stories of their first loves, first heartaches, and their dreams as big and vast as the Tennessee sky. The three of them had been close back then. As close as sisters. She watched Jenny's eyes sparkle with laughter recalling Amy's misfortune over getting caught red-handed cutting through Ms. Sherwood's garden because it was well past the hour they should have been home. Being the youngest of the three, she'd had a hard time keeping up with them. Poppy had taken a hickory switch to all of their backsides for leaving her behind. Needless to say, they never left her again. And as they laughed so hard that their sides hurt, Julie wondered when it was that they had let their closeness drift so far apart.

"So...are you ready for today?" Jenny asked.

"Not really. Is anyone ever ready to see their little girl get married?" Julie looked out across the sun-drenched waters. The lake reflected the sky like a mirror. "But then, who would have thought all those years

ago, that I'd even live to see her graduate from kinder-
garten, much less be here for her wedding day?"

"I know. Ken and I were just talking this morning
about how you must be one tough cookie to still be here
in spite of all you've been through. We were all worried
sick when you found out the cancer had come back in
your lungs. I don't know how you do it, Jules...but you
just keep on defying the odds."

"Yah, you can just call me the Energizer Bunny,"
Julie said with a laugh. But her tone grew serious as she
continued, "It's been a rough road and no one's been
more surprised than me. But you know, it's all God."

"It certainly is." Jenny, too, had briefly drifted away
from her Baptist roots when she went to the University of
Tennessee but had recently found her way back, much to
her parents' relief.

They sat in silence, listening to the sounds of the
waves splashing along the shore...both lost in their own
thoughts...their own memories.

A lot had happened to Julie since the original diagnosis. Three years after her mastectomy, her faith was
rocked to the core when Denise, a close friend of many
years, lost her battle with breast cancer. All of a sudden,
breast cancer seemed to be everywhere, like a plague.
Why had God healed her and yet so many others died?

For the first time since her mastectomy, Julie had
struggled with the fact that she was a survivor. Several
years would pass before the first and last thought of the
day was not about the disease that had so unwittingly

invaded her body and her life. Fear and doubt were often constant companions. It became a daily struggle to keep faith alive and her fears in check.

Then, nine and a half years later, just six months before she would have been declared cancer-free, a spot was detected on her lungs during a routine chest X-ray. The diagnosis dealt a devastating blow. The breast cancer had returned. Her faith was once again tested.

Julie tried not to look at statistics, strained not to focus on the percentages that grimly separated the survivors from those whose fate was less fortunate. Instead, she searched for her journal of healing scriptures, now filed away at the top of a bookcase, and once again found comfort and courage in between its pages. Strength and hope inscribed in every word. The lobectomy was the most excruciating surgery she'd ever experienced, much more painful than even the mastectomy, and the grueling recovery took much longer. For days, she was confined in the ICU, hooked up to monitors and machines. The pain, devastating. The medication so strong that she was unable to cry. Remarkably though, it had now been twenty-three years since the original diagnosis, and thirteen years since it metastasized to her lung. Her doctor now calls her his walking miracle.

"Well, I guess I'd better get going before we both fall asleep," Jenny laughed, stretching her legs in front of her before standing up.

Rinsing out the glasses in the sink, Julie handed them back to Jenny. "Thanks so much, Jenny. I'm really glad you and Ken are here. It means more to me than you'll ever know."

"Oh, you don't have to thank me. I feel like Zoe's my daughter too. I wouldn't have missed it for the world. When did you say we're supposed to meet downstairs again?"

The clock on top of the T.V. said 11:34.

"We're meeting down there at 3:00 so that we can get to the church in time to take plenty of pictures beforehand."

"Sounds good! Is there anything I can help out with?"

"No, I think we've got it covered."

"Let me know if you think of anything."

"I will. Thanks, Jenny."

"Sure thing, Agent Rock Candy."

"Over and out, Agent Snoops." Laughing, Julie closed the door behind her. It was so good to have her cousins here. Since losing her parents, Jenny and Ken were the only family she had left, outside of Amy and the girls.

Julie's hand lingered on the door knob.

Something positive had come from her journey with cancer. It was the joy of discovering life all over again. Every new morning was a gift yet to be opened. She no longer took a single breath for granted. A lot of people go through life without appreciating the small wonders around them: the rays of a sunset, the beauty of a sun-flower, the sound of rain on a metal roof, the song of a bird, the warmth of a fireplace, and the love of family and friends. It was all exhilaratingly new, as though she was discovering everything for the very first time.

But in the middle of her newfound joy, another side—a dark side—gripped her too. For months after the surgeries, Tony had been wonderful. She couldn't have asked for a more supportive and loving husband. However, as the years passed, he seemed to grow more and more distant. The more she tried to explain how much she needed love, the less and less he had showed it. The harder she tried to communicate and express her needs, the further he pulled away. Their marriage had become a dance between two strangers. Gradually, she started to withdraw, and they began to drift apart. Julie resented Tony's apparent ambivalence. And so, ten years after the mastectomy, and five years of sporadic marriage counseling sessions, she summoned up the courage to file for divorce. It had been an agonizing decision, but one that she rationalized by telling herself that they'd both be happier. She needed to know that it mattered to someone else that she was alive.

Years later, there were still unanswered questions. After all this time, Tony remained a mystery. He never had been one to show his emotions—whether they were sitting on the couch cheering for his favorite football team, or in a heated argument, Tony kept his thoughts and feelings to himself. There was a disconnect. Julie found it exhausting trying to break the invisible barrier that prevented them from enjoying a deeper intimacy and connection, and so eventually she'd stopped trying.

Julie knew he cared about her though. When she was sick, Tony was the first one to run to Walgreens to pick up a packet of Thera Flu, or when she was in the hospital it was his shadowy figure she always recognized in her groggy, drug-induced state. Julie knew he loved her, he just couldn't show it and that was the paradox of it all. It both angered and frustrated her. And also made her sad at times...very sad. Perhaps more for the unrealized potential of what their relationship could have been, than the acceptance of what it was. He couldn't have been a better father, though. And through the years, they'd remained good friends.

Glancing at the clock, she realized she'd better get a move on. Their hair appointments were scheduled for 12:00 p.m.

In the quiet, she talked to her mom and dad, thanking them for loving and supporting her. For giving her strength when her strength was gone. For believing in her, when belief in herself was failing.

Raising the side zipper on the dress, she gave herself a once-over in the mirror. For a brief second, she saw her mother standing behind her. It was the morning of her wedding to Mark, and she was zipping up her dress. Her mom's platinum blond hair shone like an angel's. She'd smiled at her, giving her a gentle hug. Julie turned around, half expecting her to be there, and in the emptiness she closed her eyes and could still feel the warmth of her embrace.

Julie picked up her small clutch on the chair and turned to leave. The door shut quietly behind her. It was now her turn to zip up her daughter's wedding gown.

— —

"Hey, Mom," Zoe answered the door, as though it was just another day. Her smooth olive complexion and hazel eyes that picked up the green in her tank top showed no sign of the frazzled nerves Julie knew had to be lurking underneath. "Almost ready!" she said in a sing-song voice as she turned back toward her bed, where she was in the middle of stuffing her things inside the striped zebra handbag delicately emblazoned with the word BRIDE in Swarovski crystals.

"Can you hold this?" she asked, thrusting her veil and zebra bag into Julie's hands. She pulled out the hotel key from her purse and turned to open the door.

"Hold on, Zoe. There was something I wanted to do before we started the rest of our day."

Julie placed the veil and the zebra bag on the bed and gave her daughter a hug. She held Zoe in her arms for a minute, the way she had when Zoe was little.

"You okay?" Zoe asked softly.

"I'm just swanky doo," Julie grinned. Zoe pulled back and rolled her eyes at her mom. The funny saying meant absolutely nothing to anyone but them. From the time she was three, "swanky doo" had been Zoe's version of "hunky-dory." "I love you so much," Julie said, holding her daughter's face in her hands.

"I know, Mom. *Stop it*...you're going to make my makeup run," Zoe said with a laugh while simultaneously wiping away a few stray tears.

"Okay, okay!" Julie said. "Let's get you married." She locked the door behind them.

Allie and the other girls bounded down the steps from their second-story rooms, all voicing their wishes on how they hoped their hair would turn out for the day. Julie refrained from telling them that she'd be more concerned about their form-fitting dresses zipping up after the insane amount of pizzas, pastas, and gelato they had consumed over the past five days.

At the bottom of the stairs, Allie turned and was surprised to see everyone waiting. "Hello, soon-to-be Mrs. Thompson," Allie teased with a wink before engulfing her sister in a hug. "Wow! You look awfully calm," she said as she pulled back, her blue eyes casting a skeptical glance at Zoe. If Allie could raise one eyebrow like her sister, it undoubtedly would have been arched at this moment.

"Don't let looks fool you. My stomach's in knots," Zoe moaned.

⚊ ⚊

The rest of the afternoon flew by. The months of preparation had resulted in a flawless wedding. Zoe's dream had come true. From the hundreds of votive candles that lit up the dark chapel like fireflies on a hot summer night to the countless lilies and roses that permeated the space with their sweet English garden aroma, the wedding had a magical aura. As "Ave Maria" floated throughout the medieval church, Julie glanced over at Tony, who was clearing his throat, an obvious attempt to ward off any unwanted displays of emotion. Julie had known it would be hard on him. This day. All those droopy-eyed, pancake mornings of Care Bear cartoons and endless games of rough-puff, gone in a flash. Saturday mornings and two little feet on top of his, dancing around the living room to Neil Diamond's "Sweet Caroline" were no more. Seemingly vanishing in an instant.

Julie wondered if Tony knew, *really knew*, how much she'd loved him. That when she'd said yes all those years ago, she'd said it without a moment's hesitation. Without a fleeting thought of Mark. She'd said yes to Tony Cortisi on those sandy shores of Panama City with everything she had left in her.

She wondered if the cancer hadn't happened, would they still be together? Would the things unsaid have seemed so loud?

Mark, the uninvited guest at Zoe's wedding, returned. Julie was growing increasingly frustrated with herself for letting the excitement at the prospect of seeing him in a few days for the first time in over thirty years dominate her thoughts. And other than the phone call from him twenty years earlier, she'd been mostly successful in resolving her relationship with Mark Jennings, relegating him to where he belonged, in the far recesses of her mind. But just as hearing his voice eight days ago had jostled her world, his phone call twenty years ago had left Julie questioning both her life and her marriage.

27

San Antonio, Texas
December 1987

With a thump, the last bag of groceries hit the kitchen counter. Less than thirty minutes until I was supposed to pick up the girls from school. No time to spare. If the pork chops were going to be ready for dinner that night, they had to be marinated and in the fridge before I left. I pulled out the Pyrex dish and plopped it down on the counter. The phone rang. I hastily went to answer it in the off-chance that it was Tony calling from one of his remote destinations.

"Hello?" I answered, out of breath.

"Julie?"

The voice on the other end caused me to stop dead in my tracks. Mark? Almost twelve years had passed since I had last talked to him and the sound of his voice catapulted me back to San Diego.

"You there?"

"Yes," I responded, barely above a whisper. The weight of my thoughts was overwhelming. Leaning against the wall, I slid down to the floor.

"It's Mark."

There was a lull while I fumbled to find the right words.

"Well, hi!" I said, swallowing hard, trying to remember the last time we spoke. I couldn't. "It's been a while!" My pulse quickened, as it always had at the sound of Mark Jenning's voice.

"Is this a good time?"

"Sure. But I have to leave to pick up my girls in about ten minutes."

"You have girls?"

"Yes...I have two."

He paused, "I thought you couldn't have any kids."

"I thought so too...but I have two beautiful surprises."

"How old are they?"

"Three and seven."

"Wow!"

The mundane line of questioning seemed odd after all these years, after all that had happened. He knew so little about me now...about the woman I had become. A mere ghost of the innocent, idealistic girl he had met all those years ago. Life had changed me. He had changed me. Fighting for my life had changed me, in ways that he would never understand.

This day and this phone call had played out in my dreams countless times over the years. A thousand thoughts and feelings sent my head racing to keep up with my heart. It was as though twelve years hadn't passed, and all the buried emotions were suddenly resurrected, encompassing every part of me with an all-consuming force. Ten years of trying to move on now seemed to go up in smoke with one phone call.

"How'd you get my number?"

"I called your parents and your mom answered. Wasn't sure if she'd give me your number, but I'm glad she did," Mark said. "So, how are you doing?"

"Really good. How are you?" I asked.

A short silence followed before Mark replied, "Doing okay." He cleared his throat. "I'm going to cut right to the chase, Jules. I've done a lot of stupid things in my life, but letting you go was the dumbest by far. Not a year goes by that I don't think of us on December 20th."

My throat tightened. I wondered if he'd been drinking. That was usually what precipitated this kind of raw transparency. But the truth was that even after all these years, December 20th resurrected a fusion of sweet and sorrowful memories for me too.

"That was one of the happiest days of my life," I responded, honestly.

"Speaking of being happy," he continued, drawing a sharp breath. "...are *you* happy?"

The question was loaded. I couldn't believe he had just asked me that. But then again, Mark was always blunt, so his bold question should have come as no surprise.

"As happy as anyone I guess. And you?" I made the snap decision not to tell him about the cancer and I didn't let on that April had filled me in about Lana, Mark's new wife, either. She had moved in lock, stock, and barrel five months after I moved out, even before our divorce was final. And according to April, Lana Parsons wasn't the type to care, either. He didn't bring her up, and neither did I. And I certainly wasn't willing to give him the satisfaction of knowing that I had asked about him.

"I've never stopped thinking about you," he said softly.

A hushed quiet settled between us. I didn't know how to respond. "Same here," I finally responded, truthfully.

"I'm flying into NAS Corpus Christi in two weeks." He paused as if silently calculating what to say next. "And I was wondering if you could possibly meet me...there are some things I've really wanted to talk to you about for a while now...of course if you can't, I'll understand."

"No, no, I want to... I just have to see if I can arrange it with the girls is all." Conflicted emotions raced through me. "Can I let you know on Thursday?"

"No problem."

I searched for a pen and paper as he gave me his number.

"Got it," I said.

Another awkward pause filled the line as though neither one of us wanted the conversation to end.

"Jules?"

"Yes."

"It's really good to hear your voice again."

"Yours too, Mark."

I had imagined this day for so long, and yet it played out very differently. There was a softness in his voice that I hadn't anticipated.

As we said goodbye, I put the phone slowly back on the cradle and sat on the cold tile floor, trying to absorb what had just happened. It felt surreal. Had Mark Jennings really just called me after all these years?

The clock in the foyer chimed three times, and reality came rushing back. I was ten minutes late to pick up the girls from school.

The pork chops would have to wait.

— ~

Over the next twenty-four hours, I wrestled with the idea of meeting Mark in Corpus. Knowing good and well how the reunion would go. Mark and I had dealt with more than our share of problems in our brief marriage; *that* was undeniable. But as many problems as our relationship had back then, a lack of passion was definitely not one of them. Meeting him would certainly be playing with fire. And my head went dizzy just thinking about it. The crazy, love-sick, riveting, all-consuming feelings bubbled up from their dormant state.

That night, I opened the closet door and fumbled around in the dark for the light switch. There it was on the top shelf, along with all the other memorabilia of my life that I didn't know what to do with. The once pearl-white album, now slightly yellowed with time. The pages tattered and worn around the edges. The pictures inside, somewhat faded. A time capsule of dreams and broken promises. Clutching it to my chest, I blew off the top layer of dust and switched the light back off.

Setting the album on the couch, I gingerly opened it. The album held pictures that had been cried over and studied dozens of times before. One by one, I slid each picture out of its plastic sleeve: the picture taken that first night at the Navy Ball, the afternoon we'd gone to see the Washington Monument and gotten soaked at the surprise downpour, the neighborhood pool party, the picture I'd snapped of Mark on our honeymoon when we were both enjoying the complimentary bottle of champagne left on our doorstep, the day we'd gone tobogganing with his brothers, and one of the many nights of duckpin bowling.

Finally, tucked safely behind a picture toward the back of the album, I found what I was looking for. The last snapshot off an old roll of film that had mysteriously reappeared out of nowhere.

Most of the roll was from an impromptu Fourth of July block party hosted by April and John. But one of the photos, the very last one, was the image that had become emblazoned in my mind and seared in my heart. The black night ignited from the static light of sparklers. Someone had snapped it when we weren't looking. Candid, unposed. My favorite kind of picture. The thirty-millimeter film managed to illuminate the spark between two twenty-two-year-olds that flamed brighter than the fireworks. Over the years, I would pull out that picture in the stillness of the night, after homework was done, teeth were brushed, and bedtime prayers whispered. Remembering.

I put the pictures down on my lap and closed my eyes. Images of the note with the flight attendant's phone number I had discovered in Tony's flight bag years ago and the unanswered questions surrounding them were quickly becoming the *only* justification I could dredge up for moving forward with this meeting that would only end one way.

It was almost impossible the next day to concentrate on our normal routine. Putting orange juice in Zoe's cereal and pouring bleach into the load of colors were hopefully the only results of a major distraction. If Tony was home, he surely would have noticed my uncharacteristic behavior. But, as usual, he wasn't. Which, in and of itself, suddenly became part of the problem. And Mark, the only solution.

All of this inner turmoil took place under the radar while I continued on autopilot with life as normal. From the carpools, to soccer practice, to arguing with

Allie over why she had to have another pair of cleats when I had just purchased a pair last month. All the while, the conversation with Mark played in the background.

The years had worn down the sharp memories of why I had left until they were dull and surprisingly irrelevant. The heated, passionate scenes of those first few weeks together in San Diego played out in the rear-view mirror of my mind like a mirage in the desert.

Tony would be home on Sunday. Which, if I dropped off the kids on Saturday with Mom and Dad, would give me plenty of time to drive to Corpus and get back in time to pick Tony up from the airport the following morning. It was simple. Too simple. *Nothing* in my life was *ever* that simple.

For two days I wrestled with questions, temptation lurking in the secret places of my heart. The indecision reeling inside started to feel more destructive than any answer. Forty-eight hours passed before I picked up the Bible. It was the last thing I did in search of an answer, when it should have been the first. *Was I ever going to learn?*

I retrieved it from my night stand, and it immediately fell open to Proverbs 4: "Watch the path of your feet, and all your ways will be established. Do not turn to the right nor to the left; Turn your foot from evil."

The answer became clear. I had too much to lose. And nothing to gain.

28

Varenna, Italy
June 15, 2008

The venue they had chosen for the reception was a small and obscure villa, frequented mostly by the locals. A friend of Zoe's had discovered it on a recent trip when she'd accompanied her parents to Italy. Villa San Lucas was nestled against the shores of Lago de Como, white lights were intertwined in the arbor above, and lanterns with votive candles were suspended from the citrus trees that bordered the perimeter of the patio. Tall candelabras were adorned with white roses, lilies, and Swarovski crystals that reflected the light. Julie exhaled. It was such a huge relief to see how perfectly everything had come together—a flawlessly romantic setting that bloomed from countless hours of planning, long-distance phone calls, and ceaseless on-line messaging.

But, gazing at it now, it had surpassed her expectations. And as anyone who knew Julie could attest, that was a near impossible feat. Now she fully understood why Zoe had insisted on dragging everyone over four thousand miles to get married. Sitting at the table, Julie made a conscious effort to try and safely tuck the memories of tonight away so that she could recall them long after the wicks on the candles had burned down, long after the glasses of wine were emptied, long after the dream had become a memory.

The rustling of the palm trees swaying in the breeze that blew off the lake made a shuffling sound that reminded Julie of the nature relaxation tapes her mother would play to calm her spirit. All the afternoons when Julie had dropped by unexpectedly for a visit and would catch her mother sitting in her Tiffany blue chair, Bible opened on the stand beside her, hands folded, eyes closed, while she rocked back and forth to the soothing sounds of waves breaking along the shoreline and seagulls squawking in the distance. A pang of longing struck again, until Julie shooed it away like she always did, instead focusing on the wait staff hard at work, clearing away the settings from guests who had already retired to their rooms.

It seemed hard to believe that after a year of planning, the "I dos", the four-course dinner, the cutting of the Italian wedding cake, and the rounds of toasts, that it was all over. Looking down at the flickering candle in front of her plate, she took another sip of the sparkling champagne. Why was it that the things one enjoyed most in this life went by the fastest? Julie would have liked to have grabbed hold of this moment, held on to it, and not let go. But life isn't like that, and time has a way of slipping quietly, methodically through one's fingers.

The red rose petals were still scattered across the cobblestoned steps where Zoe and Travis had excitedly darted off for their honeymoon in Venice. Tony and Julie were the last two to leave, and after paying the vendors, they strolled down to the water's edge, neither of them ready to let go of tonight, for that would mean letting go of Zoe.

Looking over at Tony, Julie was reminded of the day Zoe was born. She had looked so much like Tony that the only thing missing was a mustache. Even the nurses had a good laugh. She'd said an extra prayer that day, thanking God for her second miracle. Her second blessing.

After several minutes, she and Tony started to talk and talk. Of days long since passed, but still fresh in their minds. They reminisced about the funny memories from Zoe's childhood: about the time she had pointed to the statue of Jesus on the grounds of the Sisters of Oblate Seminary and in her three-year-old earnestness said, "Oh wook, Mommy, there's God!" How she'd made up her funny little songs about her sister "ChaCha," as she had affectionately referred to Allie. They always thought that the name would stick—and they wouldn't have minded if it had. And of course they could never forget the countless times she'd carted Gigi, their miniature toy poodle, up and down the steps in her plastic grocery cart, but not before tying up Gigi's ears and stuffing them under her cabbage patch doll's bonnet. An effort that only served to win total disdain for their mischievous younger daughter from their much-adored family pet. Their little girl who had loved life, seizing every second of it, was now embarking on her own.

"Well, Jules, tomorrow's gonna come pretty early. Think we should call it a night?"

What Tony said was practical, but he was *always* practical. Julie knew that he was right. She knew that the sun streaming in through the curtains at seven o'clock the next morning would feel way too early. And that she would undoubtedly be blindly groping for that first cup of coffee. But this was their last night in Italy. Was this really the time to be practical?

"You go on up," Julie said, observing Tony's bloodshot eyes. "I'm not quite ready."

"You sure?"

"Yeah."

"You did a great job, Jules," Tony said, giving her a peck on the cheek before heading back to his room.

"Thanks," Julie responded, watching as his shadowy figure retreated into the darkness.

The moon briefly disappeared behind a cloud, then peeked out again even brighter than before, spotlighting the waves as they lapped at the shoreline. Julie found a seat on a smooth rock. The breeze coming off Lake Como floated soothingly through Julie's hair. In two days, Mark would be expecting a call from her. The decision she had made not to meet him in Corpus all those years ago had been the best one. But what about now? For years, the door he had opened haunted Julie more than the one she had closed. But that was twenty years ago. Her life had changed in ways she couldn't have predicted. And who was she really kidding? From the second he had asked the question, deep down, Julie already knew the answer. They say there's a time for everything. She believed that. Maybe, this was finally their time. This time, she had nothing to lose...

The next morning came too early, and the cup of coffee at the hotel had not provided the remedy she had hoped for. Bleary-eyed, Julie dragged her red carry-on bag down the endless tarmac. One of the advantages of flying with Tony was that because of his seniority, they were usually able to sit in first class, a perk she never valued as highly as she did now. Stretching her aching legs out before her, Julie closed her eyes as the plane taxied down the jet way and slowly lifted into the air. The takeoff had always been her favorite part of flying, despite the fact that Tony had informed her when they dating that the takeoffs and landings were the most dangerous parts of any flight. She looked down at the town of Milan as it became smaller and smaller. Another ending.

"Mom," Allie said as she tapped her on the shoulder from the row behind her. "You must be a thousand miles away. Your favorite song is playing." She passed her mother the iPod. Both girls had always had a way of sensing when she was down, so as she put the headphones on, it came as no surprise to hear "Both Sides Now" by Judy Collins.

Looking down on the white puffy clouds that seemed to be standing perfectly still as the plane glided among them, the words filtered through the headphones: *"I've looked at clouds from both sides now, both up and down and still somehow, it's clouds' illusions I recall, I really don't know clouds at all…I've looked at love from both sides now, both win and lose, and still somehow, it's love's illusions I recall, I really don't know love at all."*

In fifteen hours, Flight 724 from Milan would be touching down in Chicago, and reality would swiftly rush back into all of their lives. But for now, Julie leaned back against the seat, closed her eyes, and listened to Judy Collins sing the words that at this moment felt like the mantra of her life.

29

San Antonio, Texas
June 19, 2008

Placing the steaming cup of Dunkin Donuts decaf on her desk, Julie settled into the black leather office chair and warily scrolled through the 234 emails vying for attention in her inbox. Half of them were flagged as urgent, but they would just have to wait. The only urgent thing on her mind right now was calling Mark. And it couldn't be put off any longer. Those nervous, butterfly feelings were as intense at this moment as they were over thirty-four years ago when she had returned to her dorm to find Dottie's note pinned to her bulletin board. Of course this time, the questions were very different. What would he look like after all these years? Would she even recognize him? And what would he think of her? Was he still married?

"You have that background check on Peters completed yet?" her boss asked, poking his head through the small crack in the door.

"Almost...just waiting to hear back from Harris County."

"Found anything on him?"

"Nope. Looks like he's a clean slate."

"Great. Let me know when you hear from Harris and we'll shoot your report over to the McGraw firm."

"Will do." And with that, Clark disappeared.

She buzzed the receptionist. "Nancy?"

"Yes, Ms. Cortisi—"

"Please hold my calls."

"No problem."

"Thanks."

She pulled open the drawer where she had stashed Mark's number and picked up the phone.

"Jennings," he answered in his characteristically self-assured tone.

"Hi, Mark. It's Julie."

"Hey! How was the wedding?"

"Beautiful, but exhausting. And the punishment for those ten days off is already taking its toll."

"That bad, huh?"

"Between my emails and the jet lag, I'm already looking forward to the weekend. So, when and where do you want me to pick you up?"

He seemed completely taken off-guard by her uncharacteristic boldness. "I was hoping you'd ask that," he said. Julie could hear the smile in his voice.

It was next to impossible to get much work done the rest of the day. But she did manage to pull herself together long enough to finish the reports that had deadlines looming. She told herself that it would be good to get her mind off of everything and to think about something else...anything else.

Sitting across from him at the Palmita Mexican Cantina, Julie desperately tried to recognize the man she'd left all those years ago. He had changed a lot. But one thing that hadn't changed was his devilish grin. What else could she have possibly expected after all this time? Hushed murmurs from muted conversations being played out all around them within the dimly lit room seemed more appropriate for married couples or impressionable first dates. Neither of which described them.

After ordering a bourbon and Coke for himself and a strawberry margarita for her they settled into easy conversation. The kind of conversation reserved for couples who had been together long enough to finish each other's sentences. That was exactly how her dream had begun. But not at all how it ended.

"You look great, Jules. How on earth do you manage to never change?" He leaned forward on his elbows, his full lips remained open and slack as a smile danced in his blue eyes as though he was looking at her for the first time. "It's crazy...I feel like I'm twenty-one again."

Mark studied her expressions carefully. The look on his face was hauntingly familiar. An insatiable craving that couldn't be satisfied by anything on the menu. It made Julie slightly uncomfortable and excited all at the same time. Like the first time they'd met.

But they weren't twenty-one anymore. And the years had brought with them many undeniable changes.

"It was real, wasn't it?" His eyes clouded over as he cast a look downward, squirming in his chair. He cleared his throat as though trying to clear away the memories.

"So how's Freckles? Is she married? She must be in her late forties by now. Wow, that's a tough one to swallow!"

Mark always did have a soft spot for Amy. "Freckles" was the pet name he'd affectionately assigned to her little sister from day one.

"Yep, she's forty-eight now, married with two kids. Todd is eighteen and Callie just turned fourteen last week. They're great kids."

"What about your parents?"

"Oh," she stammered, her heart sinking. "We lost Daddy ten years ago and it'll be four years next month since Mom died.

"That's hard, Jules. I'm sorry to hear that."

"Thanks," Julie said, drawing in a sharp breath and looking down. "It was tough," she said, her voice cracking. "But losing a parent never is easy, is it?"

"No, it's not," he said. "Your parents were good people, Julie. Kind."

A frown wrinkled his forehead and he reached across the table to take both of her hands in his.

Briefly, Julie turned her attention to the couple sitting in the corner. Their fingers were intertwined affectionately. That had been them once.

Mark's broad shoulders were now squared back in defiance of any weakness he had shown earlier. But Julie saw through him. How odd. It had taken all these years for the tables to turn. But turn they had. The control, the power he'd once held over her was gone. She was now the one holding the winning hand. But there was no victory here.

He stared blankly into his near empty glass. He absent-mindedly clanked the melting remnants of the ice, his thoughts far away. Once again he looked up at her, this time his eyes betraying his tough facade.

"Jules, I've thought a lot about everything that happened between us, the ways I hurt you. The way it ended. And I'm really sorry for everything." he said.

"I know you are."

"I never meant to hurt you," he continued. The words that Julie had desperately longed to hear all these years, now seemed to be the final strokes on their canvas. A beautiful painting, once clouded by tears, whose meaning was unattainable, whose depth and emotion would never fully be known.

"Can you forgive me?" he asked with genuine remorse.

"I already did, Mark" Julie answered honestly. "Years ago."

"I guess we'll never really have closure, will we," he said leaning back.

"Probably not," she conceded. "To me, that's the saddest part of it all."

It was clearly evident that time had changed them both, in more ways than one. Yet the flame still burned. Inextinguishable. Like the lingering embers from a smoldering fire, ready at any moment to crackle back into a blaze. He reached across the table, his fingers touching hers in rediscovery.

In the soft candlelight of the restaurant, Julie recognized a sorrow in his eyes—a sorrow reflected in her own. The kind that comes from decades of suffering a *Romeo and Juliet*-type love story, one that tragically, neither of them had been able to fully move beyond after all this time.

As their conversation continued, and the nerves and anticipation began to die down, Julie realized something for the first time in her life. She had put Mark so high on a pedestal that every man who came after him had been forced to climb a mountain they didn't even know existed—a mountain whose summit was impossible to reach. And yet, the person sitting across from her at that moment was really quite unremarkable. Quite ordinary. Three decades of her life had been spent immortalizing and longing for a man who, when it came right down to it, was very similar to every other man in her life. Julie leaned back in the padded booth and watched him, as though she was an observer at the table instead of a participant. Gray peppered his hair, the way his father's had all those years ago. Weathered, ruddy skin now surrounded those eyes she so clearly remembered every time an image of him would pop into her head.

The self-assured, cocky, handsome, Top Gun fighter pilot was no longer there. In his place sat a man who had seen more than his fair share of heartache—a man who seemed to be burdened down with a heavy load of regret.

"So you're not married. Is there anyone special in your life?" he asked, leaning forward.

"Not really. I haven't wanted to venture down that road again. I'm pretty happy these days on my own."

"Really?" he asked, bewildered, as though it was the most astonishing thing he'd ever heard.

"I'm not saying that if the right person came along, that I wouldn't give love another shot. But it would have to be the *right* person." Julie turned the tables on him. "So, what about you?"

"I remarried five years ago. She's great, and we get along...I mean, not like *us*—I gave up on finding that years ago...thirty-four to be exact," he added with a wink. "But I do love her."

"I'm happy for you, Mark." And as the words left her lips, Julie realized that she really did mean them.

He squirmed in his chair, put his napkin down on the table, and looked up at her once again. "Why didn't you want to meet me all those years ago in Corpus?"

Julie folded her hands, resting her chin on them, blankly staring at the brightly colored bottles that illuminated the glass shelves behind the bar area, as she searched for an honest response. An answer to a question she'd turned over in her mind many times. "I don't know, Mark. I guess for a lot of reasons...but mainly I had too much to lose."

"Did you ever regret it?"

"Sometimes," Julie answered truthfully. "Of course I did."

The end of their relationship had left both of them scarred. Wandering through the decades, trying to put the pieces of a broken dream back together the best way they knew how.

They sat in the booth for over three hours, closing the place down with memories of the good times. That night as she dropped him off at the hotel, Julie Whitaker said goodbye to Mark Jennings for what she knew in her heart would be the last time. One last goodbye. One final embrace.

Pulling out of the Marriot hotel, a light rain started to fall. It would take at least half an hour to get home. The moaning of the tires and the swishing of the windshield wipers droned hypnotically. It was late. One o'clock in the morning. Julie switched on the radio to her favorite oldies station. The song "In My Life" came floating across the airwaves...

> There are places I remember. All my life, though some have changed. Some forever not for better, some are gone, and some remain, all these places have their moments, with lovers and friends, I still can recall, some are dead and some are living, in my life, I loved them all...

The evening certainly hadn't transpired the way she'd anticipated. Mark Jennings. The name alone for so many years had conjured up images of flagrant, steamy nights in San Diego. The man who for over thirty-four years had held her heart captive with suffocating what-ifs.

The windshield wipers picked up speed as the rain evolved into a steady downpour. She couldn't tell which was falling faster, the rain or her tears. Were they from sadness? Relief? Or maybe both?

By the time Julie pulled into the driveway of her Cape Cod-style home on River Oaks Drive, complete with its gray rustic shingles and fresh white paint, the rain had subsided enough to graciously leave her mostly dry as she darted up the short sidewalk. The cozy cottage on the banks of the Guadalupe River had previously been a summer getaway for a family from Massachusetts. And one year ago it had become hers. She found the thirty minute drive to be therapeutic—a chance to unwind after a long day.

Tossing her keys in the brown wicker basket on the kitchen counter while simultaneously pressing play on the answering machine, she half-listened to the three messages while opening a can of Tuna Supreme for Toby, who waited patiently for his second meal of the day. Toby, her orange and white Calico, rubbed up against Julie's leg in gratitude. The first message was from Jenny, excitedly exclaiming that the pictures she had taken from the wedding had turned out "fabulous!" and she was hurriedly transforming them into a scrapbook of sorts for Zoe. Next was Allie, just "checking in," which really meant, "how'd it go with Mark?" She always had been the nosier of the two. And the last was from Nina, her neighbor, reminding her about the weekly Bunco game. In two years, Julie had attended a total of four nights at best, and still Nina called every Sunday.

The warm evening breeze felt refreshing as Julie settled into the wooden back porch swing, her legs tucked tightly underneath, staring up at the overcast sky. The wind whispered all around while the shimmering moonbeams peeked through the rustling leaves of the tall maple trees, leaving silver trails that illuminated the well-worn path to the river. A sated Toby jumped up on the swing and nuzzled close to her, curling up into a ball and purring affectionately. A nightly ritual they'd both grown to treasure over the past couple of years. Two summers had passed since he'd showed up on the front porch, making his way into her heart, almost as swiftly as he had forged his way into her home.

She needed some time to reflect on her meeting with Mark. But, she reminded herself, 5:30 would come early the next morning. How had she arrived at this place: this place of contentment, this place where she truly loved and accepted herself—in spite of all her perceived mistakes, or maybe because of them? The answer at times was baffling. But now sitting here, reflecting on her life, she realized that Jesus had been there all along. Wiping every tear. Carrying her when her strength was gone. And guiding her steps when she lost her way. Julie's dad had mailed her that one-way ticket home all those years ago. But Jesus had purchased the ultimate one-way ticket home over two thousand years ago. And one day when it was her time, her Heavenly Father would be waiting there with open arms welcoming her home, just like her daddy had all those years ago.

One thing was certain—somewhere along the way Julie had changed. There was no resemblance from the woman she was now, to the once starry-eyed young woman of her youth. Perhaps it had begun the moment she stepped onto that plane in San Diego for the final time. Or the day she put down the bottle of Quaalude and picked up a Bible instead. The day she said yes to Tony Cortisi on the sandy shores of Panama City. Or perhaps it had been the day she looked into each of her daughter's eyes for the first time or held her parents' hands for the last. The times Julie had clung to faith and hope in her darkest hours, when letting go would have been a much easier choice. Every time she'd smiled, when she wanted to cry. Quietly, steadily, she had grown a little stronger in all those days, all those moments, and the countless forgotten ones in between.

And somewhere in the dark beyond, the river bubbled gently as it slid over the rocks, careening around the bend, flowing onward in its endless quest to the sea.

> *God is our refuge and strength, an ever-present help in trouble. Therefore we will not fear, though the earth give way, and the mountains fall into the heart of the sea, though its waters roar and foam and the mountains quake with their surging. There is a river whose streams make glad the city of God.*
>
> *Psalms 46:1-4 (NIV)*

Acknowledgements from Kristie Hardy:

I cannot even begin my acknowledgements without giving Jesus Christ, my Lord and Savior, all the glory. Without His unfailing love, mercy and forgiveness, this book would not even have been possible. To my wonderful parents whose exemplary Christian walk was an inspiration to us all. I wouldn't have made it through this life without your love and support. To my two beautiful daughters who are living proof that we serve a miracle working God. To my husband, whose understanding and patience is unmatched. And finally to my friends, who each in their own unique way, contributed to the final outcome of this book, and whose dreams and expectations sometimes exceeded my own.

Acknowledgements from Cate Hardy:

To my amazing husband and two beautiful children, who over the past eight years that this book has been in the works, patiently gave me the time and space to fulfill a dream. As I often say, I am blessed far beyond anything I deserve. To my mother, who courageously decided to share her story, in the hope that it would encourage and inspire others in their own journey. To my parents and grandparents, whose Christian foundation is still the ground on which we trod. To my sister, who has been an instrumental part of this journey and whose own story is woven throughout our book as well.

Both of us would like to acknowledge the talented editors who over the years have worked with us to polish our manuscript. To Diane O'Connell, whose tough love critique of our very first draft forced us to make an about-face and helped turn this book into the enjoyable read it is today. To Susan Malone, who took the time to convey the fundamental principles of good writing. And last, but certainly not least, to David Ferris, whose final look through was the icing on our cake.

Our acknowledgements would not be complete without applause for the amazing Danielle Maait, who brought our vision to life with the beautiful cover she created.

Made in the USA
Charleston, SC
14 September 2016